A servant leader is patient and kind.

A servant leader doesn't envy others or boast.

A servant leader is not proud or rude,
does not insist on having his or her own way.

A servant leader does not become easily angered,
doesn't hold grudges or keep a list of people's past mistakes.

A servant leader is never happy with any form of evil,
but is always searching for truth.

A servant leader always protects others,
trusts others, and always hopes for the best.

A servant leader never gives up.

—1 Corinthians 13:4–7,
paraphrased

STRENGTH
IN
SERVANT LEADERSHIP

By the Same Author . . .

The Communicator's Commentary —
James, 1, 2 Peter, Jude

PAUL A. CEDAR

STRENGTH
— IN —
SERVANT
LEADERSHIP

WORD BOOKS
PUBLISHER
WACO, TEXAS

A DIVISION OF
WORD, INCORPORATED

Library of Congress Cataloging in Publication Data

Cedar, Paul A., 1938–
    Strength in servant leadership.

    Bibliography: p.
    1. Christian leadership. 1. Title.
BV652.1.C43   1987   253   86–28249
ISBN 0-8499-3086-3

Printed in the United States of America

7898 BKC 987654321

This book is lovingly dedicated
to my father, the Reverend
Carl Benjamin Cedar,
who has been my first and
foremost model of servant leadership.

CONTENTS

FOREWORD

My dear friend—and deeply valued pastor—
Paul Cedar, is not only a most effective teacher of
biblical concepts but is a man who models them con-
sistently for his congregation and for those hosts of
people touched by his ministry.

"Servant Leadership" is a currently popular
theme a good bit like Mark Twain's weather—we
discuss it a good deal, but don't do a whole lot about
it. However, Paul Cedar brings into sharp focus the
basic scriptural principle of leadership which serves,
as perfectly exemplified by our blessed Lord, Jesus
Christ, and shares how this concept is essential for
both the "professional" clergy as well as for laymen
who seek to be effective and biblical in their service.

Not only do we find prayer guidance and most
helpful instruction in this carefully prepared and intensely interesting manual, but included are necessary words of warning and caution. This is a message

which desperately needs to be heard and heeded in a day when it seems accountability is lacking in so much of our Christian society. Dr. Cedar has the unique—and insightful—ability to "hold our feet to the fire" in this necessary role in leadership effectiveness which truly honors the Lord. Here is an appropriate word in season for all of us who want to bring the highest honor and glory to the One whom we love and serve.

The illustrations and highly personal experiences that Paul uses herein are readily recognizable by us all. The practical, helpful suggestions for meeting and relating to various leadership styles provides a part of the charm of this book. Candidly, I can think of no leader—or potential leader (which Cedar insists is all of us)—who would not be helped and challenged by this carefully thought-through and scripturally documented material. It has been worked through the crucible of the author's experience. And—again—I have witnessed it operative in his life, experience and leadership. May God help each of us to lead with the "servant heart." In this attitude both God himself and those with whom we share are blessed.

TED W. ENGSTROM
President
World Vision

PREFACE

THE PREPARATION OF THIS BOOK HAS SPANNED MANY
years of ministry and learning. Although I have not
mastered the art of servant leadership, I am in the
process and believe it is time for me to share the
insights that God has given me thus far in my journey.
I pray that in reducing to paper these principles of
servant leadership, I will be helped to apply those
same principles more effectively to my own life. I am
sincere when I say that I long to be a faithful servant
leader for Christ and his Church.

In addition, I hope that these principles and insights will be of help and encouragement to scores of
readers by enabling them to become more effective
servant leaders. Also, I trust that others will be motivated to write additional volumes about servant leadership which will help all of us who are committed to
follow Jesus as Lord and to lead as his servant leaders.

13

14

I wish to express my deep thanks to the brothers and sisters who have assisted me in this labor of love. Many of their names are mentioned in this book while others are not. My specific thanks to Floyd Thatcher who has been a marvelous example of a servant of Christ while serving as editor of this book. Thanks to Marion Matweyiw, my secretary; to Mark Cedar, my administrative assistant; to my dear wife, Jean; to Dr. Carl Tracie and the many others who have participated in the preparation of this volume. Above all, I acknowledge the love, grace and motivation of our Lord Jesus Christ. It is my deepest desire to be his faithful servant and to do his will!

CHAPTER 1

SERVANT LEADERSHIP:

Who Needs It?

Although our talents, personalities and gifts may vary, I believe that Scripture teaches us clearly that there is one leadership "style" which is uniquely Christian. It has been given to us by the Lord of the Church. He has modeled this leadership style and commanded us to do likewise.

HARRY GLADSTONE IS THE SENIOR MINISTER OF A large urban church that for many years has enjoyed a well-earned national reputation for its dynamic ministry. However, Harry only recently assumed his present role after serving for twelve years as Minister of Christian Education.

Harry's predecessor, Dr. Alvin Speakes, was an energetic and gifted man who served as pastor of the church for twenty-three years. He was a strong, highly respected leader who was in charge every one of those years—a classic example of a benevolent dictator. Dr. Speakes could best be described as a "super minister" who gave firm leadership to a "super church."

In a way, Harry became the senior minister by default. When Dr. Speakes died very suddenly from a heart attack, everyone in the church had been stunned. However, within a short time, a search committee was commissioned to find an interim senior minister. At the same time, they asked Harry to serve as interim pastor since he was very dependable and highly respected by the congregation.

After months of searching for "Pastor Right," the committee was hopelessly deadlocked; they couldn't agree on a candidate. Finally, someone suggested the obvious, "What about Harry? He's doing a great job as interim; everybody in the church loves him. Why not ask him to be the permanent Senior Minister?"

This suggestion was received enthusiastically by the congregation, and the official call was extended to Harry. After a time of prayerful consideration, Harry and his wife, Martha, felt they had the Lord's guidance to accept. Both of them realized that Harry faced an awesome task in attempting to succeed Dr. Speakes. But Harry was committed to give it all he had—and Martha was dedicated to assist him in every possible way.

However, within a few months, everything began to go wrong. After twenty-three years of authoritarian leadership, the church didn't like Harry's democratic style. Factions had formed, and a power struggle was fermenting among the church lay leadership as well as the pastoral staff. People whose ambitions had been frustrated for years were asserting themselves in a rather ruthless manner. The church was fast becoming paralyzed, and Harry seemed helpless to do anything about it.

Storm clouds of dissension hovered over the church. There was a bitter taste in the air. Harry knew that the Holy Spirit could not work in such an atmosphere. What should he do? Should he attempt

to assume the "benevolent dictator" style of his predecessor—or should he admit that he had failed, give
up, and resign? These were the crucial questions that
needed answers.

In desperation, Harry took a week's vacation so
that he and Martha could get completely away for an
uninterrupted time of prayer and searching the Scriptures in an attempt to find some answers. They had
to get relief from the intense strain that blocked out
any word from the Lord. Then, as one day followed
another, a calming peace filled their hideaway like a
beautiful surprise. The Lord seemed to open up the
Scriptures in a new way for them. And Harry made
a discovery that was not only to change his own life
but would also transform the life and ministry of his
great church. For the first time, Harry discovered a
biblical model for "servant leadership."

SERVANT LEADERSHIP IN BUSINESS

While Harry was making his exciting discovery,
one of his parishioners was facing a great challenge
in his own life. John Steelman was a bright and gifted
junior executive for a major financial firm. At the age
of thirty-three, he had worked his way up the corporate ladder to a significant leadership position. With
all of his success, however, he faced one major problem—that of getting along with his colleagues—
especially those who reported to him.

John was an incisive and decisive producer. He
set goals and accomplished them with great regular-

ity—usually ahead of schedule. And he used people effectively to accomplish those goals. That was the source of his major problem. The people who reported to him didn't like him or his leadership style. They complained that although John claimed to be "religious," he was a manipulator and didn't really care about people; in their opinion his only concern was for goals and projects.

One day the president of the company called John to his office for a conference. His conversation was friendly but to the point. He felt John had great potential for becoming a senior executive in the company, but first he had to learn to work more effectively with people. At the same time, he needed to assume a leadership style that would develop the talents and skills of his colleagues—not make them feel used and abused.

That evening, a dejected John discussed what had happened with his wife Sally. As they worked through the problem, John began to see that he was not only falling short as an executive, but he was failing as a Christian leader. While his friends and family knew him as a loving and caring person, his reputation on the job was that of a scheming manipulator and a ruthless achiever. John and Sally began to wrestle with the question of how he could "live out" his deep commitment to Christ and still be an effective executive. Slowly they began to see that John's answer could only be found in a practical day-by-day application of the biblical principle of "servant leadership."

SERVANT LEADERSHIP IN THE HOME

Mary Alvarez was another member of Harry's church, the single mother of three teenage children. Her husband had been killed in an automobile accident, and she was left with the awesome task of caring for her children. Mary had experienced periods of anger toward God and had asked some difficult questions: Why had God done this to her? How could God expect her to be both mother and father? Where was God when she needed him most?

After emerging from weeks and months of both anger and grief, Mary had a marvelous experience of emotional and spiritual healing. This relief came as she spent time seeking the Lord in Bible study and prayer, talking about her feelings with caring friends, and in counseling with her pastor. Through all of those experiences, she began to discover some insights regarding "servant leadership" which applied to her role as mother and family head.

This is not to say that Mary doesn't have some low moments of frustration, loneliness, and grief. But, most of the time, Mary and her children share life together in the joy of her discovery!

SERVANT LEADERSHIP IS FOR EVERYONE

Harry, John, and Mary are representative of different people, in different situations with different needs—and yet they each experienced a common need—the need for a Christian leadership style that would work in their particular situation!

Now, as a rule, we think of church leaders as ministers, board members, or Sunday school teachers—and they are. It is true that those positions are often the key leadership roles in a church. But in a very practical sense, most all of us as Christians are in leadership roles in one way or another—in church, in our family settings, on the job, or in our social and service involvements. For example, a teacher of a fifth grade Sunday school class needs the same biblical guidelines for leadership as does the pastor of a church, an executive of a business, or a parent of a Christian family— or the coach of a little league baseball team. And the good news is that God has given us guidelines to help us be effective leaders in every situation of life!

I have already referred to this leadership style as "servant leadership." It was both taught and modeled by Jesus Christ. He was and is the master servant leader. And each of us needs his style of leadership as we attempt to be effective Christians in every part of our own lives. We need to lead as Jesus did. He has entrusted to us a unique and wonderful style of leadership that is edifying to everyone involved in the process—to both the leaders and the followers. We need to commit ourselves to fulfilling the command of our Lord—to be servant leaders!

The church today is in dire need of such leaders, and that same concern is being felt in other segments of our society. In fact, the servant leadership style is fast becoming recognized as effective in the corporate and business world.

For example, the response to Robert Greenleaf's fast-selling book, *Servant Leadership,* has been most impressive. He refers to his book as "a journey into the nature of legitimate power and greatness." And Greenleaf goes on to say, "The great leader is seen as servant first, and that simple fact is the key to his greatness."[1]

For primarily pragmatic reasons, many business and industry leaders are recommending a form of "servant leadership"—simply because it works! But there is an even better reason for us to become servant leaders—our Lord commanded it as absolutely essential for the accomplishing of his kingdom. The Gospel writer underscored this truth as he pointed out the model Jesus himself gave us: ". . . the Son of Man did not come to be served, but to serve . . ." (Matthew 20:28).

A few years ago I was invited to lecture as a guest professor at one of the leading theological seminaries in the United States. When I arrived on campus, I was delighted to discover that the chairman of the Department of Practical Theology was a long-time friend whom I had not seen for a number of years.

While we were walking together across the campus, he said something which amazed me. It came without warning and with a great deal of concern on his part. In summary, he said, "You know, Paul, I believe that without realizing it or without attempting to do it, we are training most of our students to be failures as pastors of local churches."

As I was recovering from my initial shock, he continued, "You see, we are using as our models for church ministry the superchurches of the world which are served by superpastors. The truth is that most of our young people will serve small churches of 200 people or less. They will never be superpastors, nor will they serve superchurches. I fear that when they serve what they perceive to be ordinary churches, and when they do not become superpastors, they will feel that they have failed. It should not be so. We should be using other models for success and effectiveness in training for pastoral ministry."

I agreed with my friend that day—and I continue to agree with him. Nowhere in the Bible is the success or effectiveness of our leadership determined by size. Whether our church or business or home is large or small is not of primary importance. What is important is our use of the abilities and resources which God has entrusted to us. For example, special rewards are not offered by the Lord to those who are unusually gifted. The teaching of Scripture is that "to whom much is given, much is required." And in the parable of the talents, Jesus taught us that we must be faithful stewards only of the gifts and resources which we have at our disposal.

SERVANT LEADERSHIP IS PRACTICAL

This is very practical teaching. A parent with five children needs to care for those children just as effectively as the parent who has only one child. An employer who has several thousand employees has the same responsibility to them as does a small businessman who has one part-time person working for him. And a pastor of a 5,000-member church needs to care for his flock just as lovingly as a pastor who has a congregation of 100 members.

At the same time, it is important for each of us to realize that we, as Christian leaders, can't be cast into any single mold. God gives different talents, gifts, and personalities to his leaders, and it is this diversity that expresses God's creativity and love. We are not "carbon copies" of one another. This truth comes through in living color as we are reminded of our biblical models—Peter did not lead in precisely the same way as did Paul, and Joshua didn't try to be Moses. But each were servant leaders.

Although our talents, personalities, and gifts may vary, I believe Scripture teaches us clearly that there is one leadership "style" which is uniquely Christian. It has been given to us by the Lord of the Church. He has modeled this leadership style and commanded us to do likewise. It is the model of "servant leadership."

Please understand that I don't pretend to have mastered this style of leadership. Like many of you, I am in the process of growing and learning how to do it. Let me share some of that personal process with you to help you better understand why I have come to believe so strongly that "servant leadership" is vitally important—and why I am convinced that it works in any leadership situation.

During my years of involvement in ministry, I have been privileged to serve churches of various sizes and sociological settings. I grew up in a Presbyterian manse. My dear father served as the pastor of several churches in Minnesota and South Dakota. Then, while attending college in South Dakota, I served for two years as a youth pastor and choir director in a small city church. After being married just before my senior year in college, I became the pastor of a delightful rural church that had three families—with a total of seven church members.

During the next several years, I ministered with two large parachurch organizations and then was pastor of two mission churches—one in a fast-growing suburb of Chicago and the other in the booming Orange County area of Southern California. Each of these churches had small beginnings but experienced rapid growth.

Next, I served as the interim pastor of a wonderful but fractured urban church just a few miles from downtown Los Angeles. Following that I was Pastor of Evangelism and Executive Pastor for five and one-half years, serving with Dr. Lloyd Ogilvie at the First Presbyterian Church of Hollywood. Now as I write, I have had the joy of serving for a number of years as the Senior Pastor of Lake Avenue Congregational Church in Pasadena, California—a church described by some as a "superchurch."

I have shared this brief summary of my own pilgrimage with you for one reason. Through all of these experiences over a period of some twenty-five years (which have included ministries and churches of many shapes and sizes), I have come to believe that the same basic style of leadership is needed in every situation. In my opinion, every Christian minister, Christian parent, Christian coach—indeed, every Christian involved in any vocation or responsibility of leadership—has one common need: to be a "servant leader!" A leader who serves as Jesus served; a leader who leads as Jesus led! I believe that God is calling all of us to become *servant leaders!*

CHAPTER 2

SERVANT LEADERSHIP:

Where Do We Begin?

Servant leadership is much more than a leadership style that we learn to "act out" and master like other management styles. Servant leadership begins with the heart—with our attitude, with our motives.

Your attitude should be the same as that of Christ Jesus . . . making himself nothing, taking the very nature of a servant . . ."
—Philippians 2:5,7

HARRY GLADSTONE FACED THE LEADERSHIP CHAL-
lenge as the pastor of a large church; John Steelman
struggled to find an effective leadership style as a
young executive; Mary Alvarez worked at learning
how she could successfully lead her children as a
single parent. Each of them found "servant leadership" to be a central element in solving their personal
leadership crisis.

Their common discovery of servant leadership
ties in with my own experience. Several years ago,
while serving as pastor of a wonderful church, I felt
that God was leading me to a new place of service. My
wife Jeannie and I were confronted with an agonizing
decision. There was a great spirit of love between us
and the members of our congregation. They didn't
want us to leave, and we didn't want to depart. But,
as it became clear to us and them that it was the Lord's
will for us to go, we made the difficult decision. A
spirit of unity prevailed throughout the church. In a
wonderfully moving service of prayer and sharing,

31

the congregation lovingly commissioned us for our new ministry.

Three months later the glow of that warm experience was gone. I was involved in one of the most painful "desert experiences" of my entire life. Things were not going well. For the first time in my life as a minister, I experienced a deep sense of frustration and failure. Embarrassed and discouraged, I felt the Lord had failed me at the very time I was trying so hard to be faithful and obedient to him.

I was no longer a "white knight in shining armor"—the brilliant young Christian leader everyone wanted to follow. Instead, some people were questioning my leadership ability and there were some who seemed to be working against me. Discouraged and hurt, I wanted to retreat to the safety and comfort of the loving congregation I had just left. But, of course, I couldn't do that. And so I became disillusioned and angry. Finally, in my despair, I called out to God to rescue me.

He did! He reached out to me with love and forgiveness. He began to teach me some things about myself—and specifically my leadership style. I found that a great deal of my leading was being carried on in *my* own strength and with *my* human wisdom. I sensed that God was lovingly "calling me up" to a higher level of leadership—that he was preparing me for ministry which could not be accomplished without his presence and power. Then he began to open my eyes to my need of being a servant leader in every area of my life.

This brought me to a confrontation with some vital questions: How do we become servant leaders? Where do we begin? Who will teach us how and show us the way? What is the first step that I need to take?

THE ATTITUDE OF JESUS

In searching for the answers, I was reminded of what Paul had to say about leadership in Philippians 2. He stated that servant leadership must begin with our attitude. If we are to act like servant leaders, we must have the attitude of servant leaders—the attitude modeled by Jesus Christ. Paul's description of the attitude of Jesus Christ provides a wonderful model for us as we seek to be servant leaders.

Even though Jesus was God in human form, he didn't capitalize on that. Instead, to finalize his plan of salvation, he emptied himself; he made himself nothing, humbled himself and became obedient—even to death on a cross. And, if that were not enough, he took upon himself the nature and attitude of a servant. God became our servant! Jesus described this incomprehensible act in the following way, ". . . the Son of Man did not come to be served, but to serve, and to give his life as a ransom for many" (Matthew 20:28).

For me, then, the first answer to the "How Do We Begin" question is that we must have the very *attitude* of Jesus Christ. I realize that most of us will respond immediately by stating it is impossible to do it. We are not like Jesus. We might desire to be, but we aren't—and we know it! And because we know it, frequently we use our humanness as an excuse or an alibi. Our attitude is wrong, and we stop trying. Or, if we do try, we experience failure after failure and finally give up.

I believe the Lord wants us to see that the only way we can become like Jesus Christ is to "give up" our attempts to do it on our own and commit ourselves to him. Paul reflects his own attitude in graphic language when he says that we should "die" to self so that we can become spiritually alive in Christ. And he was not merely suggesting that initial dying to self when we become Christians. Rather, he was saying that this is a day-by-day, moment-by-moment lifestyle. He wrote, "I die every day!" And then, to make himself perfectly clear, he proceeded by asserting to his astonished readers, "I mean that . . ." (1 Corinthians 15:31).

That is to be our attitude if we are to be authentic servant leaders. Servant leadership is much more than a leadership style that we learn to "act out" and master like other management styles. Servant leadership begins with the heart—with our attitude, with our motives.

I am convinced that it is virtually impossible to be a servant leader if we are not first servants of Jesus Christ and, therefore, filled and empowered by the Holy Spirit. I don't believe this is merely a theological or religious theory. Our beginning point is that moment when we invited Jesus Christ to be the Lord of our lives and received the indwelling and controlling of the Holy Spirit. We can never learn to "act" like Jesus Christ without first surrendering to him and allowing him to live his life in and through us.

We have been invited by God himself to live as he lives, to serve as he serves, to lead as he leads. That is a profound challenge that can only be met as Christ through the power of his Spirit lives in and through us.

A Desert Experience

In order for most of us to have an attitude change, God lovingly leads us into what we may call a "desert experience." We see this model taking place frequently in Scripture. For example, when Moses attempted to lead the people of God with his own strength and ingenuity, he killed the Egyptian guard who had been beating a Hebrew slave. Instead of showing appreciation or acknowledging Moses as a potential savior, another Hebrew slave who saw what happened asked, "Who made you ruler and judge over us? Are you thinking of killing me as you killed the Egyptian?" (Exodus 2:14).

When Moses realized someone had seen him murder the Egyptian, he literally ran into the desert and ended up in Midian. There he met Jethro, married one of his daughters, and became his father-in-law's chief shepherd. Moses, the adopted son of Pharaoh's daughter, who grew up in the splendor of Pharaoh's palace and was probably trained for a significant role in Pharaoh's administration, failed miserably. He ended up leading sheep in the back side of the desert.

But it was there years later that God spoke to him through the burning bush. At that moment God called him to leadership. He chose him for one of the most difficult tasks of leadership in the history of mankind—to lead the Hebrew slaves out of bondage in Egypt to the Promised Land. Moses' first reaction was one of fear and possibly failure. However, he finally submitted to the word of the Lord!

The years that Moses had spent tending sheep in the desert prepared him for his new assignment. He no longer succumbed to the temptation to lead in his own strength or to develop his own plan of action. Instead, he became totally dependent upon the Lord for strength, for wisdom, for strategy, and for day-by-day guidance. Moses had a dramatic change of attitude. He now became a servant of God and looked to the Lord for leadership.

Moses wasn't the only person to face a "desert experience" with the Lord. Jesus himself spent some forty days in the desert in preparation for his ministry. David had to hide in the desert for many months to escape King Saul's wrath before becoming the King of Israel. Elijah fled from his victory at Mount Carmel to escape to the desert from Jezebel who was determined to kill him. Jonah's "desert experience" was spent in the belly of a large fish! And Saul, who became the apostle Paul, spent a significant period of time in the desert following his conversion as God prepared him for his powerful ministry. God used each of those "desert experiences" to mold the character and leadership skills of his servants.

I am not suggesting that you seek a "desert experience." But I am urging you not to resist such an experience if it comes. Instead, we should see it as a wonderful love-gift from our Lord.

It would be nice, of course, if we could avoid such desert experiences. But it seems that most of us begin to learn the principles of servant leadership within the crucible of some painful experience such as Moses had in Midian, or Harry Gladstone with his church problems, or John Steelman in coping with leadership failure, or Mary Alvarez in experiencing parenting needs—or Paul Cedar in recognizing his own inadequacies. Our loving Lord wants to meet us where we are. He longs to teach us how to become effective servant leaders as we allow him to give us his attitude of love and humility. And, with that wonderful gift will come some special opportunities and challenges.

How do we begin? As we turn our lives over to the Lord and are empowered and controlled by the Holy Spirit, we will be enabled to handle some very special challenges.

SWIMMING AGAINST THE STREAM

As servant leaders we will soon discover that we are swimming against the stream. The concepts of servant leadership are contrary to much of what most of us have learned about leadership and management from such highly respected sources.

As we explore servant leadership from a biblical perspective, we will find that it is "out of tune" with much of the most highly respected management systems popular today. Jesus expressed it this way, "You know that the rulers of the Gentiles lord it over them, and their high officials exercise authority over them. Not so with you. Instead, whoever wants to become great among you must be your servant, and whoever wants to be first must be your slave" (Matthew 20:25, 26).

As you can readily see, servant leadership is an apparent paradox and is contrary to our logical thinking. On the surface, it simply does not make sense. How can I be a leader if I am the servant or the slave of the very people whom I am attempting to lead? How can such a leadership style be acted out in the "real world" in which there is so much evil and competition and abuse of power?

That seemingly paradoxical statement is closely related to another well-known statement made by Jesus: "For whoever wants to save his live will lose it, but whoever loses his life for me and for the gospel will save it" (Mark 8:35). Without a doubt, Jesus is speaking to us about the "ownership" or control of our lives. Who "owns" me? Who is in control of my life? Who decides what I will do or where I will go or what I will say? Who leads me? Whom do I follow?

The average person who is totally honest would have to admit that he or she is in charge of his or her own life. I am responsible for myself. I make my own decisions about what I will do, and where I will go, and what I will say. I lead myself, and I follow that which I enjoy—that which is fulfilling and/or what makes me feel good.

This is the human way. But Jesus comes to us and says that it isn't his way. His way is different. If we are to follow him, we must say "no" to ourselves—we must deny ourselves and take up our cross (daily) and follow Jesus (Mark 8:34). We are to *serve* rather than *be served*. We are to follow Christ with all of our hearts and souls, and minds and strength—and invite people to follow us only as we follow him!

We begin by accepting the challenge to live as God created us to live; to lead as he wants us to lead. We move from our own personal agendas to the agenda of our Lord. Without a doubt, this is a great challenge.

THE IMPORTANCE OF MOTIVE

I have also come to believe that we begin our adventure of servant leadership with a re-examination of our motives. God is not merely concerned with "what" we do, he is greatly concerned with "why" we do things. As you will remember, Saul, the first king of Israel, was taught this truth in a most dramatic fashion. He was not leading as a servant leader in the way God desired. Instead, he was leading in the natural style. He was "doing his own thing" in his own way—and he was using his power for personal gain.

This led to his disobeying God very directly by saving everything that was "good" when he had defeated Agag and the Amalekites (1 Samuel 15). The Lord sent the prophet Samuel to Saul to ask, "Why did you not obey the Lord?" and to pronounce sentence upon him: "You have rejected the Word of the Lord and the Lord has rejected you as king over Israel" (v. 26).

Then, because God rejected Saul, the Lord sent Samuel to anoint the new king of Israel. As Samuel followed the Lord's guidance, he was led to the house of Jesse in Bethlehem. When he saw the oldest son, Eliab, he was so impressed with his physical appearance, he thought that Eliab must be the Lord's anointed one. But the Lord said, "Do not consider his appearance or his height, for I have rejected him."

The Lord continued by saying, "The Lord does not look at the things man looks at. Man looks at the outward appearance, but the Lord looks at the heart" (1 Samuel 16:7). What a profound statement—not only about Eliab or Saul or David, but about all of us! God is concerned primarily about our hearts. He uses leaders whose hearts are right with him. He knows that as human beings, we tend to look for external leadership traits. We are impressed by leaders who are handsome, strong, and physically appealing. Eliab and Saul were both physically attractive. Even the godly prophet Samuel was impressed with their appearance.

But God sees beyond the externals to the heart. He sees not only the "what" of our lives but the "why." He understands that overt human conduct and behavior flow from the heart. When the heart is right, the behavior is right! Jesus stated this truth emphatically when he declared, ". . . out of men's hearts, come evil thoughts, sexual immorality, theft, murder, adultery, greed, malice, deceit, lewdness, envy, slander, arrogance and folly" (Mark 7:21, 22).

Our motives are determined in our hearts. Unfortunately, our natural motives are selfish—that is the very basic manifestation of sin in our lives. Jesus said that the sinful behavior of our lives flows from the motives of our hearts.

If we are to live as he lives and lead as he leads, our hearts must be possessed by something better than the natural. We need our hearts to be filled and controlled by Jesus Christ. And when he controls our hearts, he gives us a new capacity for living. His motive becomes our motive—and his motive is always *love!*

How do we begin the adventure of becoming servant leaders? By opening our lives to God and allowing him to reshape our attitudes. Sometimes it requires a "desert experience" and sometimes it doesn't. However, the action is always the same—we die to self and become alive to God. He fills us with the Holy Spirit—and with the Holy Spirit comes the gift of love.

That love becomes the hallmark of our attitude and the very essence of our motives. Servant leadership begins with the humble, loving attitude of Jesus.

I have a pastor friend who is not very handsome or dynamic. He is a below average speaker and is lost in the world of administration. Yet, he is an effective leader for one primary reason. He loves people. His attitude is the humble, loving attitude of Jesus. He serves people with the obvious motive of love. And, as he loves, he is loved. Scores of people love, trust, and follow him. In short, his attitude is right.

Recently Gordon Aeschliman, who is the editor of *World Christian Magazine*, penned the following words which I believe should be the prayer of all of us who seek to be servant leaders.

> *Don't give us blessings—give us grace to be unquestionably obedient to Your every last command and desire.*
> *Don't give us status—give us a place to serve.*
> *Don't give us things for our use—use us.*
> *Don't give us a mansion to live in—give us a springboard to take Christ's love to the whole world.*
> *Don't give us good jobs—put us to work.*
> *Don't give us pleasure—give us perspective.*
> *Don't give us satisfaction—teach us sacrifice.*
> *Don't give us entertainment—enable us.*
> *Don't give us good salaries—give us strength to do Your will.*
> *Our great joy in life is in pleasing our Lord—and there is no other joy comparable.*[2]

CHAPTER 3

SERVANT LEADERSHIP:

Love Is Essential

God does not give us power to be used for our own ends or desires. His power is entrusted to us so that we are motivated to serve God and others with the love of Jesus Christ and the power of the Holy Spirit!

A new commandment I give you; Love one
another. As I have loved you, so you must love
one another. All men will know that you are my
disciples if you love one another.
—John 13:34–35

LOVE IS CENTRAL TO THE CHRISTIAN LIFE, AND LOVE is central to servant leadership! When love is our motive, it is seen in our attitudes and actions. Jesus indicated that this lifestyle of love would be the litmus test for our discipleship. He contended that everyone would recognize us as his disciples because we would love one another in the same way that he loves.

Although love begins in the heart, it is manifested in practical, observable ways. For example, the apostle Paul instructs husbands to love their wives in the same way that Christ loves the Church (Ephesians 5:25). At this point, a good question would be, "How does Christ love the Church?"

Paul answers that important question by saying, "As he gave himself up for her." In other words, Christ demonstrated his love for the church by giving himself for it—by "serving" it. From this, I understand that God's model for the way in which husbands are to love their wives is to *serve* them. Now, that won't sound very desirable to our male-oriented society.

Tragically, this teaching has been ignored throughout much of church history by a male preference for another part of Paul's teaching in Ephesians which states that wives should *submit* to their husbands. Unfortunately, the focus on service has been often down-played along with Paul's insistence that there should be a mutual submission in love to one another out of reverence for Christ (v. 21).

I believe that both teachings are vitally important if we are to understand the biblical concept of love in marriage and in servant leadership. When we love one another as Christ has loved us, we will submit to one another in love, and we will give ourselves to one another just as Christ has done for us!

Since the word "love" is used and misused so frequently in our modern society, I think it is important for us to be certain of what it means here. The writer of 1 John gives us a simple yet profound definition when he writes, *God is love!* And from the teaching of Jesus we learn that God's love is unconditional—we can't earn that kind of love; we don't even deserve it!

But, as most of us know, the Bible gives us some additional insights for defining love in very practical, measurable terms. If we are to be servant leaders who have love as our basic motive, just how do we translate that into our day-to-day actions? After all, it is one thing to say that we should act as Christ would act, love as he loved, submit as he submitted, and serve as he served. But it is quite another thing to follow through and live out those noble words in a practical, "hands-on" manner.

LEADING WITH LOVE

I believe an exciting model for "leading with love" is found in Paul's marvelous teaching in 2 Corinthians 13. There we find a graphic picture of how love is to look and behave in all of life—and especially in servant leadership. In fact, it is not inappropriate for our purposes here to substitute the words "servant leader" whenever the word "love" or "charity" is found in 2 Corinthians 13. As we do, we will discover a practical and workable definition of servant leadership. Let me show you what I mean with the following paraphrase of verses four through seven:

> *A servant leader is patient and kind. A servant leader doesn't envy others or boast. A servant leader is not proud or rude, does not insist on having his or her own way. A servant leader does not become easily angered, doesn't hold grudges or keep a list of people's past mistakes. A servant leader is never happy with any form of evil but is always searching for truth. A servant leader always protects others, trusts others, and always hopes for the best! A servant leader never gives up.*

There we have a vivid description of the life of the ultimate servant leader—Jesus Christ. And that description provides a measurable model for each of us who want to be servant leaders. To be sure, if we were expected by God to "pull off" this kind of leadership style in our own strength, we would be destined to fail. To love and lead and serve as Jesus did requires the strength and power of Christ himself! We can't do it without him. However, as the apostle Paul reminds us, "I can do everything through him who gives me the strength" (Philippians 4:13).

But the Good News of the gospel is that we can be servant leaders! We can love as Christ loves. We can be what God wants us to be and do what God wants us to do—with his enabling power through the Holy Spirit. That is God's promise to each one of us.

Paul shared this promise with young Timothy when he wrote, "For God did not give us a spirit of timidity, but a spirit of power and love and self-discipline" (2 Timothy 1:7). Interestingly enough, the love of God and the power of God go together. Or, perhaps a better way to express it is that they "come" together. Both are readily available to us. As Jesus prepared to conclude his earthly ministry, he took his disciples out to the Mount of Olives and gave them this promise, ". . . you will receive power when the Holy Spirit comes on you" (Acts 1:8).

Luke's narrative in the Acts of the Apostles reveals to us that those were not only our Lord's words of commissioning, they were prophetic words soon to be fulfilled. In the second chapter of Acts we read about those awesome events that took place as the Holy Spirit came to dwell within the disciples. The Spirit's power broke through their lives in remarkable ways, including the message of Peter delivered on the streets of Jerusalem when several thousands received salvation through the risen Lord (Acts 2:38).

Before those startling events which occurred on the Day of Pentecost, there wasn't any particular evidence that Peter had much spiritual power. It is true, of course, he had come to love Jesus during their time together. And Jesus had put a lot of trust in Peter, even to the point of calling him "the rock." The Lord said that he was going to build his church upon Peter and his leadership.

But on the night Jesus was arrested and faced his greatest trial, Peter let him down. It is true Peter was ready in the garden to protect Jesus with his sword. Peter wanted to do the right thing, but he didn't have the power to stand firm, and so he denied his Lord. He caved in and said he didn't even know Jesus!

Many of us can identify with Peter. We are sincere, and try to do our best, but that isn't good enough. After all, Peter was sincere, but he didn't have spiritual power until he received the Holy Spirit. It was then he moved out boldly to witness for Christ as a servant leader.

In an excellent article entitled "What Ruins Christian Leaders?" Russ Reid warns about the abuse of power. He quotes a famous senator, "When I leave my office to go to the Senate floor, an elevator comes immediately . . . reversing its direction if necessary and bypassing the floors of the other bewildered passengers aboard. . . . As I walk down the corridor, a policeman notices me coming and rings for a subway car to wait for my arrival and take me to the Capitol building. . . . At the Capitol, another elevator marked 'For Senators Only' takes me to the Senate floor."

The words belong to U.S. Senator Mark Hatfield. They are words about power—about the rights and privileges bestowed on one who has placed himself into the rarified air of Washington politics—where raw power is enshrined and seniority amply rewarded. Senator Hatfield has come to terms with his power, but he himself admits that the struggle not to abuse it never ends. Unfortunately, this arena is also filled with the stories of Christian leaders who have built tremendous ministries but who don't know how to exercise the power their creation has given them. Their early vision—with its absolute dependence on God—often has shifted to a nightmarish *one-man show.* "Unilateral 'seat-of-the-pants' decisions upstage good counsel. 'The Lord told me to do it' often becomes a pious platitude to justify leapfrogging over the wisdom of boards and committees."[3]

God does not give us power to be used for our own ends or desires. His power is entrusted to us so that we are motivated to serve God and others with the love of Jesus Christ and the power of the Holy Spirit!

Bob Toms, who is a prominent Los Angeles attorney, shared the following insights about power and servant leadership as he spoke recently to a group of Christian students: "Jesus was very candid about his power and how to be great in the kingdom. 'Whosoever will be chief among you, let him be your servant.'

"Sun Szu and Niccolo Machiavelli notwithstanding, Jesus taught an inverted pyramid of power; to be a Christian leader one must (1) humble oneself,

(2) submit to God's authority, and (3) serve those who need a shepherd. Leaders were to function from the bottom, not the top. Again, the Good News is absolute dynamite: political power, wealth, birth, race and sex are not prerequisites to this kind of power, and leadership and the competition for it is not keen, but a large group can be led from the bottom by the authentic Christian servant leader. Most of all, by few words and consistent deeds an eternally eloquent argument is made to the hearts and minds of a few men and women, and where the Word made flesh finds acceptance and 'takes,' there follows self-generating procreation of faith as natural as beggars sharing precious bread and requires no pushing or coercion."[4]

This is what Paul had in mind, I believe, when he wrote to his young protege, Timothy. Yes, in our own strength we are weak and timid. In our strength our witness isn't very convincing. But Paul makes it clear to Timothy and to us that as God's witnesses—as his servant leaders—we are to have power through the Holy Spirit.

When Paul was writing to the Corinthian Christians; he told them of the word he received from the Lord during a time of trial, "My grace . . . is made perfect in weakness" (2 Corinthians 12:9). Like Paul, we are weak, but God's power acts through our weakness and changes us from timid people to become powerful witnesses. As servant leaders, we should use the power which God entrusts to us to lead others to follow us as we follow Christ (1 Corinthians 11:1).

THE FRUIT OF THE SPIRIT

As the Holy Spirit grants us power for living and leading, he gives us other resources as well. The Scripture describes these as "gifts of the Spirit" and as "fruit of the Spirit." The fruit of the Spirit is described in Galatians 5: 22–23: "But the fruit of the Spirit is love, joy, peace, patience, kindness, goodness, faithfulness, gentleness and self-control. . . ."

I believe that all of this fruit is available to all Christians at all times. As we allow Jesus Christ to be the Lord of our lives, and as we allow the Holy Spirit to indwell and control us, the fruit(s) of the Spirit are manifest in and through our lives. These are not qualities we can develop nor are they skills we can learn. The only way to possess them is to be possessed by the Holy Spirit.

This fruit goes hand-in-hand with the power of the Holy Spirit. God does not give us power for the sake of power. He gives us power so that we can live to his glory, and so that we can influence others for his kingdom! It is important for us to understand that our personal weakness becomes an ally in advancing Christ's kingdom.

When Christ comes to live within us in the person of the Holy Spirit, we are empowered to do things beyond our personal ability. He places the treasures of his fruit and power within us. Paul states that the Lord does this for a most practical and functional reason. ". . . we have this treasure in jars of clay to show that this, a surpassing power, is from God and not from us" (2 Corinthians 4:7).

BUILDING WITH LOVE

Let's face it, as servant leaders, we will have different leadership goals whether we are leading our family members, employees, participants in social organizations, or members of a church. However, all of our goals should focus on two important principles—accomplishing the will of God and building up the lives of all those we lead. God never abuses or violates persons. He wants his servants to grow through all of the experiences that he provides for us. What builds us up builds up his kingdom. And what builds up his kingdom builds us up.

We live in a disposable society. We enjoy the luxury of throwing away paper cups and plastic plates that we use only once. We do the same with plastic spoons and cardboard milk cartons and a thousand other kinds of disposable items that are an integral part of all of our lives. We expect to "use up" things and then get rid of them. Most of us drive a car for two or three years and then trade it in for another. We expect things to be depreciated with use and to be discarded in a relatively short period of time.

Unfortunately, this mentality frequently finds its way into interpersonal relationships. Some young people "use up" one boyfriend or girlfriend after another. And many adults "hop" from one marriage to another after "disposing" of their former mate. The church is also affected. Scores of Christians have become known as "church-hoppers." They discard one church for another to satisfy their current tastes or desires.

Those of us who are called to be servant leaders face the same basic temptation—to use people as disposable objects. Our goal in leadership cannot be merely to accomplish our own selfish desires or even simply to perform a task which we may consider important or worthy. We must remember constantly that God has entrusted us with the task of building up people as we lead them to accomplish the will of God in their lives.

In Ephesians 4 Paul shares a most important leadership model with us. We will explore that model in detail later, but for the present, let me simply refer to his vocabulary in that chapter. In the second verse of that chapter Paul writes about "bearing or supporting" one another with love. That is a part of servant leadership. We are called upon to "bear or carry" one another's burdens, for that fulfills the law of Christ (which is to love one another as Christ loves us). In other words, we should be willing to help others with their problems, encourage them when they are discouraged—and to feel hurt when they hurt. Love motivates us to identify with the needs of others.

But the life of love is not only communicated by loving identification, it also needs to be expressed verbally. In Ephesians 4:15, Paul writes about "speaking the truth in love." Servant leaders need to speak the truth in love. What does "speaking the truth in love" mean? I believe it involves speaking words of encouragement and direction. At the same time it can involve words of guidance and help when a Christian brother or sister is in trouble or is caught up in some kind of sin.

Paul states that when we speak the truth in love, both the person speaking truth and the person hearing truth will "grow up" into Jesus Christ himself. What a wonderful and awesome experience! The One who is the source of all truth wants us to communicate truthfully to one another. Servant leaders need to love others so much that they will "risk" by speaking the truth in love even as our Lord speaks truth to us! And as we do, we will grow together in the grace and knowledge of our Lord Jesus Christ.

Such loving and honest communication requires a great deal of risk. I find that those I appreciate most are the people who love me enough to "risk" telling me the truth. They are my dearest, most trusted, friends. This is in stark contrast to what I would call "no risk" or "selfish leadership." Selfish leadership is destructive. It uses and abuses people like disposable objects. Each time we "use" people, we remove something from their lives. We consume rather than build; we take from them rather than give to them.

When I was in high school, the word came to us from the federal government that our entire little South Dakota town had to be moved. A major dam was to be built on the Missouri River which flowed near us. Some ten feet of water would cover the beautiful valley where the town was located.

As a result, I spent two summers working on the moving project. One summer, I spent working with a demolition crew. It was our job to destroy buildings which could not be moved. That included the beautiful high school building which was well constructed with brick and block. Much to my amazement, we were able to destroy that magnificent structure in a matter of days.

In contrast, I spent another summer on the construction crew of the new school. I had the task of serving as the "mudboy" for the bricklayers. While it took only a few days to destroy the former building, it took months and months to construct the new. As a young man, I learned a principle which is primary to all of life. Destruction can be fast and easy. Building is time-consuming and difficult.

God has called us to be builders! We have the delightful task of building with a dual role—we are builders of the kingdom of God, and we are builders of the lives of God's people. This is true regardless of the leadership role we may have. As the pastor of a church, a teacher of a Sunday school class, a leader of a scout troop, the parent of children, or a supervisor of employees, I am called to be a "builder of lives" as a servant leader. I am privileged to carry the burdens of those who follow me and to speak the truth in love so that we may together "grow up" into Christ. I am a builder for Christ as I build up others in love.

Bob Mitchell, the President of Young Life, expressed this truth very clearly in a moving letter to his constituents when he wrote, "A servant-leader is one whose message is embodied in his (her) life . . . one whose attitude speaks 'acceptance' or willingness to listen . . . one who treats people as individuals and calls them by name. These attributes seem so minor in the total definition of leadership, yet how great a difference they can make in a club kid or an adult questioning Christ's lordship, or to a fellow worker who wonders what it's all about being a Christian."[5]

Most importantly, it was the kind of leadership Christ intended for us to follow.

> *"I have given you this as an example so that you may do as I have done. Believe me, the servant is not greater than his master and the messenger is not greater than the man who sent him. Once you have realized these things, you will find your happiness in doing them."*
>
> *—John 13:15–17 (Phillips)*

CHAPTER 4

SERVANT LEADERSHIP:
Some Biblical Models

God has given us a perfect example of servant leadership. This person lived among us for some thirty-three years; he spent three of those years in intensive ministry. It is vitally important for anyone who aspires to be a true servant leader to examine the life of Jesus Christ. In all of human history, he is the prime example of an effective servant leader.

From him the whole body, joined and held together by every supporting ligament grows and builds itself up in love, as each part does its work.
—Ephesians 4:16

LEADERSHIP DOES NOT TAKE PLACE IN A VACUUM OR in a void; it takes place within a community of people. A leader cannot live in isolation; he or she must relate to other people.

Leadership roles are assumed in various ways. For example, a pastor like Harry Gladstone is called by the vote of a congregation or appointed by a bishop to give leadership to a local church. John Steelman became a leader in his business through the invitation of his boss. Mary Alvarez became the sole leader of her family because of the death of her husband.

However, in God's work in our world, it is he who decides who will lead. Scripture declares that promotion does not come from the east or west or south. Instead, it comes from God (Psalm 75:6–7). In Ephesians 4 we find a very important model for leadership within the church. It relates some basic principles which we must all understand as essential to leadership in the kingdom of God!

A Model for Leadership

Paul informs us that there are at least five leadership roles or gifts in the church (Ephesians 4:11). God gave some to be apostles, some to be prophets, and others to be evangelists, pastors, and teachers. Each of these persons had specific leadership gifts within the early church. We won't explore the function and responsibilities of each leadership gift here. Instead, we will focus on the more important question which is, "What is the common purpose of these leadership gifts?" Or, in other words, "Why does God give leadership gifts and roles to certain members of his church?"

Peter speaks to this question in his first letter when he writes that "Each one should use whatever gift he has received to serve others, faithfully administering God's grace in its various forms" (1 Peter 4:10).

Paul agrees with Peter's teaching, but is more definitive in presenting the specific way in which leaders should use their gifts to serve others. Specifically, all five of the leadership categories are charged with the responsibility of "equipping God's people." In other words, leadership within the kingdom of God does not exist merely to meet the ego needs of those who are leading. Nor do the nonleaders exist merely to be followers or to serve leaders. Quite to the contrary, the leaders are entrusted with the ministry of serving the followers by equipping them. The word equipping in the Greek text means "to make whole" or "to restore that which is missing" or to "mend that which is broken." Servant leaders are called to minister to broken, hurting, incomplete people by building, healing and encouraging them with the grace and love of Jesus Christ.

The next logical question becomes, "For what should leaders equip the people of God?" Paul states that leaders should equip the people of God in order for them to be involved in the ministry of serving others. In summary, the passage teaches us that leaders are called to minister to the followers by equipping them so that they, too, can minister. Think of the potential of that statement. For example, what a difference it would make in most of our churches if we would not expect the minister to do all the ministry of the church. Instead, he should spend a great deal of his time equipping the members of the church to be involved in ministry. That is God's plan—instead of one person being hired to do the work of ministry for us, *all* of us have the privilege and responsibility of being involved in ministry *together*.

Without a doubt, that is a description of a most unusual community of people. The church is more than a mere *organization* with leaders and followers. Instead, it is an *organism* where each member of the body is working properly in ministering to one another. Those who have leadership gifts are using those gifts to minister while all the members are using their spiritual gifts to serve both the leaders and the other members! What a marvelous experience it would be to participate in such a community.

That should be the normal experience of every Christian who participates in a local church. The church should be that wonderful and delightful place where everyone is using his spiritual gifts in serving others!

But that isn't the whole story. The Bible teaches us that through all this wonderful ministry activity, something very important happens—the body of Christ is built up! And this results in two wonderful manifestations of the unity of the body. First there is the unity in the faith and, secondly, there is the unity in the knowledge of the Son of God. Most of us realize that if leadership is to be effective, there must be unity among the participants. I have seen this phenomenon a number of times in my ministry.

When I speak of "unity," I am thinking of much more than the mere absence of disagreement or contention. In a dictatorship, for example, there is not much expression of disagreement or contention. Anyone who disagrees is usually executed or imprisoned. But authentic unity comes from the heart. If people are living in unity, that oneness begins with harmony of the heart under the control of the Holy Spirit. We often refer to this as "unity of the Spirit." It is not something which can be organized or controlled.

The church that I serve as pastor has faced some major decisions in recent years. I'm delighted to report that we have resolved most matters by a unanimous vote of the church family. That may seem too good to be true. There is no way we could organize for that kind of unity. Instead, we have prayerfully sought the will of God together. In response, he has blessed our congregation with agreement and unity.

I don't believe that such unity is the result of any one leader "knowing the truth" and serving it up in finished form for others. Instead, servant leaders attempt to get everyone involved in seeking God's will for themselves as well as for the entire congregation. And, as we pray and study his Word and seek the Lord together, God gives us a unity of heart and purpose.

Notice that Paul does not teach us to have a knowledge "about" Christ, but rather a knowledge "of" Christ. That, too, is the task of a servant leader— not merely to know about Christ but to know him personally as Savior and Lord! Only then can he or she lead his or her fellow Christians to know Christ and to grow and mature in the faith. The culmination of this important model now comes into focus: we will "become mature attaining to the whole measure of the fullness of Christ" (Ephesians 4:13).

In summary, the Lord has given leadership gifts to the church so that the leaders would equip the people of God. He did that in order for them to minister to (serve) one another. This "mutual ministry" results in the body of Christ being built up so that all the participants would reach a unity in the faith and in the knowledge of Christ. The ultimate result of this "serving" activity would be for all of us to grow to a level of maturity which can be measured by nothing less than the full stature or person of Jesus Christ himself! In other words, we grow to become more and more like Jesus!

When that goal is achieved everyone wins; no one loses! We don't take from one person to give to another. There is enough of God's love and grace and power for everyone! As servant leaders we have the joy of helping people grow to become what they were created to be—like Jesus Christ. I believe that is exactly what the Bible teaches us in the creation account when we are told we were created in the "image of God" (Genesis 1:27). Sin has distorted that image badly. Only Christ can return it to us! And he chooses to do it as we become servant leaders and build one another up to become more like him! That is the ultimate purpose of the church and of servant leadership!

A Second Model

There is another important model which we need to study. Of all the models of leadership found in the Bible, this one is the most concise as it states, "Follow me as I follow Christ" (1 Corinthians 11:1). To put it in other words, "Imitate me as I imitate Christ."

Some people believe this teaching is an arrogant and egotistical statement by Paul. In fact, I find that many ministers dislike this teaching. It tends to be intimidating; it makes us feel uncomfortable.

Is Paul teaching that a servant leader must be "perfect" before he or she can lead others? Of course not. Paul recognized that he was not perfect. In a later letter he stated, "Not that I have already obtained this or am already perfect, but I press on to take hold of that for which Christ Jesus took hold of me" (Philippians 3:12).

What Paul is saying in this model of leadership is quite different. He is speaking here primarily of "direction." I believe he is inviting his readers to follow the Lord even as he does. In other words, he is saying, "Let me help you! Follow me as I follow Christ. I will lead the way. I am Christ's servant, and he has called me to serve you as you seek to follow him." That is the statement of a servant—not an arrogant egotist.

But for most of us this is a frightening model of leadership. It requires risk and leaves us so vulnerable simply because we are asking people to watch us, to follow us, to trust us. Naturally, the assumption here is that we can be watched, followed, and trusted because of our faithfulness to the Lord.

Immediately we are tempted to emphasize that in our own strength, we are incapable of being examples anyone should follow. However, as we all move ahead together in our Christian pilgrimage, we hold each other responsible for the integrity of our life and witness. There is a mutual accountability under the Lord that holds us steady.

We need to remember the lessons of Jonestown. When Jim Jones began to be the leader of an urban church, he appeared to be a faithful and committed servant of Jesus Christ. He seemed to be inviting people to follow Jesus and to become a part of a local church that ministered to the poor and needy. However, at some point Jim Jones changed his agenda. I don't know how many people attempted to call him to accountability. But I do know that hundreds of his followers took their eyes off Jesus Christ and blindly followed Jim Jones. They followed the wrong leader, and that led to disaster.

The temptation, even among church leaders, is to go on an ego trip and to work at building our own kingdom rather than the kingdom of God. Such leaders are more concerned with their own agenda than God's. They seem to enjoy controlling the lives of other people more than setting them free through faith in Christ.

Paul warned of this tendency when he cautioned the Corinthian Christians about personality worship and about the division that comes to the church when we follow a person as our ultimate leader rather than following Jesus as Lord. He summarizes the problem by saying, "One of you says, 'I follow Paul'; another, 'I follow Apollos'; another 'I follow Cephas'; still another, 'I follow Christ'" (1 Corinthians 1:12).

Fortunately, most of us have had models of servant leaders at one time or another in our own lives. My own father has been one of those models for me. From the time I was a child, I have never doubted that his deepest desire was to do the will of God and to serve and help people. As a result, he has been deeply loved by scores of people whom he has lovingly served and in whose lives he has made an investment.

Throughout my father's ministry, he served churches in small towns in the midwestern part of the United States. In that role, there were great expectations placed upon him not only in the church, but in the community as well. I never saw him refuse to minister in any situation because it was "beneath" him. A memorable illustration of this servant attitude occurred when I was about twelve years old.

As we were walking down the main street of our little South Dakota town, we came upon a noisy group of people gathered around the town drunk who had passed out on the sidewalk. My father didn't say a word as we made our way through the crowd. He knelt down and looked closely at the unconscious man whose clothes were covered with his own vomit. Immediately the crowd started ridiculing my father. Instead of responding to their taunts, he asked me to help him get the man to his feet. We took him to his home where we cleaned him up and put him to bed.

That episode made a deep impression on my young heart and mind. There were other such instances over the years where my father was the ideal model of a servant leader to me. I will always be grateful for my dad's example.

I would encourage you to prayerfully reflect on a person who has been that kind of model for you. As you do, let me suggest several common denominators which will probably emerge. First, those persons who were models to us were not perfect people. In fact, none of us has ever known a perfect person—except Jesus Christ. From this, we should learn that God uses less than perfect people to lead others—including you and me!

There is a second insight which is vitally important. We have learned not only from the strengths and successes of model servant leaders, but we learned also from their weaknesses and even from their failures. God is not the cause of our failures, but often, after we have repented of our shortcomings and he has forgiven us, he uses even those failures as vehicles of grace to minister to others. That is a marvelous demonstration of his goodness. It is humbling to realize that people who follow our leadership often learn from our failures. That, of course, is not an excuse for us to fail. It is merely a testimony of the grace and goodness of our Lord.

Finally, we may be reminded of the fact that we have often failed adequately to express our gratitude to those dear people who have been models of servant leaders in our lives. When people assume servant roles—even as servant leaders—it is easy to assume that they do not need to be thanked or acknowledged. We tend to treat them like servants! I believe that one of the most neglected ministries in the church is that of failing to encourage and express our thanks to faithful servants of Christ. I pray that you will be prompted to take the initiative to express your love and thanks to such persons in your life if you have "fallen behind" in this important act of charity and gratitude.

God has provided models for us to follow. First, there are the models which are presented to us in Scripture. The models which we have reviewed in this chapter are two of the most helpful models available to us. I would suggest that you spend some time studying these models for yourself by doing an indepth review of both of these passages. As you study them with your mind, ask God to reveal deep truths to you regarding how you can apply these models in a practical way to your own life and ministry.

Secondly, God has provided key people in our lives who have been role models of servant leadership. Most servant leaders continue to have those persons in their lives who go on being servant leaders to them. It is like a marvelous chain of God's mercy and grace. God provides servant leaders for us as we provide servant leadership for those he has entrusted to our care.

Thirdly, God has given us a perfect example of servant leadership. This person lived among us for some thirty-three years; he spent three of those years in intensive ministry. It is vitally important for anyone who aspires to be a true servant leader to examine the life of Jesus Christ. In all of human history he is the prime example of an effective servant leader.

CHAPTER 5

SERVANT LEADERSHIP:

The Ideal Model!

The servant leader must be ready to give to others whatever God has given to him or her. The servant leader owns nothing; all he or she has comes from the Lord and is readily available to be given to anyone who needs it.

Now that I, your Lord and Teacher, have washed your feet, you also should wash one another's feet. I have set you an example that you should do as I have done for you.
—John 13:14–15

THE SETTING WAS SOLEMN. IT WAS JUST BEFORE THE Passover Feast. In just a few hours, Judas was to betray Jesus. He knew this was to be his last meal with his disciples prior to his crucifixion.

Without a word, Jesus got up from the table, removed his outer clothing, and wrapped a towel around his waist. After that, he poured water into a basin and began to wash his disciples' feet, drying them with the towel that was wrapped around him (John 13:4–5).

Most of his disciples said nothing. No one offered to help him. They enjoyed being served. Only Peter protested. The Lord used it as an opportunity to teach Peter an important lesson about servant leadership. "Unless I wash you, you have no part with me," said Jesus. Then Peter responded, "Then, Lord, not just my feet but my hands and my head as well!" (John 13:8–9).

When Jesus had finished washing the disciples' feet, he put on his clothes and returned to his place at the table. Then he asked them, "Do you understand what I have done for you?"

No one answered him. Jesus continued, "You have called me 'Teacher' and 'Lord,' and rightly so for that is what I am. Now that I, your Lord and Teacher, have washed your feet, you also should wash one another's feet." Then Jesus shared the application—for what he had both done and said: "I have set you an example that you should do as I have done for you" (John 13:12–15).

"I have set you an example!" That is one of the key elements in the life and ministry of Jesus. He not only "spoke" the truth, he "lived" it! He didn't merely tell us what to do; he showed us what to do. And he didn't merely tell us how to live; he gave us an example. He lived the life of a servant leader before us so that we could follow his example.

As he spoke to his astonished disciples on that memorable evening, he explained something about his role as an example of a servant leader when he said, "I tell you the truth, no servant is greater than his master, nor is a messenger greater than the one who sent him. Now that you know these things, you will be blessed if you do them" (John 13:16–17).

His teaching is clear. Examples are not only to be seen or even merely to be admired. They are to be imitated. Jesus was an example to the disciples and to us so that we would live as he lived. To recognize and understand the example of another person is important; but the real benefit comes from following that example by doing the same thing. Jesus is saying, "Do what I say, and do what I do. I have taught you the truth—and I have lived the truth before you. Follow my example!"

TEACHING BY EXAMPLE

We need to understand that this teaching of Jesus on the occasion of his last supper with his disciples did not take place in a void. He did not wait until after his final hours with them to begin the ministry of being an example to them. On the contrary, his was a constant and continual model of ministry. In fact, the very word "ministry" means "service." To be a minister is to be a servant.

Wherever he went during his three years of intensive service, Jesus took his disciples with him. They heard him teach, but they also saw him feed the hungry, cause the blind to see, the deaf to hear, the lame to walk and even the dead to live! He modeled servant ministry for them constantly. They did not learn theological truth in a musty classroom setting. They learned in the crucible of life. Jesus was a living example to them day by day as they followed him!

Without a doubt, this had a profound effect on the disciples of Jesus. They did not learn mere theory. They experienced and witnessed truth before their very eyes. In his first letter, Peter referred to that profound example set by Jesus when he wrote, "To this you were called, because Christ suffered for you, leaving you an example, that you should follow in his steps" (1 Peter 2:21).

Peter had not only witnessed the example of Jesus himself, Peter taught others to follow that example—even those who had never personally met Jesus, for many had become Christians after Christ's death, resurrection and ascension. Peter declares clearly that we should "follow in his steps"!

If we are to be serious about servant leadership, it is absolutely essential for us to follow in the steps of Jesus. The Lord has called us to a leadership style that is unnatural. It is a paradoxical leadership style at best. On a night in which he was hurting deeply, when he recognized that his death was only hours away and that great pain and humiliation lay just ahead, Jesus needed the love, support and encouragement of his disciples. He needed to have them minister to him at this time of great need. In a few minutes, one of his closest and most trusted friends was going to betray him—sell him for thirty pieces of silver. How he must have agonized with grief and pain.

But no one ministered to him. No one reached out to serve him. No one responded to his needs. Instead, he ministered to his disciples. He served them with love and humility. He performed the most lowly of tasks—he washed their feet—even the feet of Judas. Few of his disciples seemed to notice or even to care. Perhaps they were involved in their usual table talk. Their favorite topic was discussing which of them was to going to be the greatest in the kingdom of God. Who was going to sit on Christ's right hand and who would be on his left? Each of them seemed to feel that he was uniquely qualified for that honor.

That subject of honor was terribly important to them. They did not like the teaching of Jesus concerning his suffering and death. For months, he had been attempting to prepare them for his imminent suffering and death. But they wouldn't listen. Instead, they wanted to talk about the kingdom and the power and the glory. They wanted to be leaders in the kingdom of God. Even one of their mothers became involved in the power struggle taking place among the disciples.

The mother of James and John, the sons of Zebedee, came with her sons to Jesus to ask a favor of him. Jesus asked her what she wanted, and she replied, "Grant that one of these two sons of mine may sit at your right and the other at your left in your kingdom" (Matthew 20:20–21). What a request! Perhaps James and John were too shy to ask or perhaps they thought that it would be more difficult for Jesus to deny the petition of a loving mother. Whatever the reason, their mother asked Jesus the impossible.

He responded with truth by saying, "You don't know what you are asking." And then he spoke directly to James and John by asking, "Can you drink the cup that I am going to drink?" Without hesitation, they responded, "We can!" Obviously, they did not know what they were saying. Since they did not understand the question, they did not begin to fathom the implications of what they were asking—nor what they were contending. They had no idea what the "cup that I am going to drink" was all about.

Their eyes were not on Jesus nor were their hearts in tune with him. Their attention focused upon themselves. They wanted power, prestige and popularity. They wanted to be the greatest in the kingdom of God—and they naively assumed that they deserved it. They believed that they were the greatest—and so did their mother.

When the other ten disciples heard what was going on, they were angry and indignant. I don't believe they were angry at James and John and their mother because of their request. On the contrary, I believe they were upset because they had not thought of the idea first so that their little loving mothers could have lobbied for them! James and John had "outfoxed" them; they were "one up on them."

As the disciples were fighting among themselves like spoiled little children, each wanting his own way, Jesus called them together and said, "You know that the rulers of the Gentiles lord it over them, and their high officials exercise authority over them. Not so with you. Instead, whoever wants to become great among you must be your servant, and whoever wants to be first must be your slave—just as the Son of Man did not come to be served, but to serve, and to give his life as a ransom for many" (Matthew 20:25–28).

What a statement. Can you imagine that? The disciples were arguing about who deserved to be the greatest in the kingdom of God—and Jesus talked to them about being servants! Our first human response may be, "Boy, did they get what they deserve!" But when we begin to apply the teaching of Jesus to our own lives and personal situations, we may lose our enthusiasm very quickly for the model he gave us of leadership. In this remarkable story Jesus gave us three important principles of his leadership style.

1. *To become great, you must be a servant.* The first principle that Jesus teaches is directed toward those who want to become "great" in their lives, and that is most of us. We all want to be above average, better than the ordinary. As a boy growing up in northern Minnesota, I used to enjoy playing the game we called "King of the Mountain" with my friends. The object of the game was simply to gain the place of supremacy on the top of the snow pile by pushing everyone else off.

In one way or another, most of us have been playing that game since we were children. We long to be the greatest and the best at whatever we do. Often that requires pushing other people "off the mountain" by using power plays or politics or money or intimidation—or whatever else it may require. Power plays may include gossip or slander or merely "tearing another person down" to "build ourselves up."

In the real world, many people have attained positions of leadership by exerting political power or using their family name or buying a position by "calling in the chips" on some past favor they have done for someone else. That is how it is done out there. And so it was natural for James and John to think it might work with Jesus. But it didn't. And it won't work for us.

Jesus said that if we want to be truly great in his eternal kingdom, we must become willing servants.

We must be actively involved in serving him and others. His teaching seems to imply that the more effective we are in serving, the greater we will be in his kingdom. That is a marvelous paradox for truth; people who are willing to become servants really don't care much about being considered "great."

2. *To be first, you must become a servant.* The second principle that Jesus shared focuses upon those who want to be "Number One." The principle is much the same as being great. However, in becoming great, there is room for several people. The disciples understood that. They were chosen by Jesus to belong to an elite group of just twelve disciples. Without a doubt, they saw themselves as great within God's kingdom. They were among the top twelve in all the world.

But that wasn't enough! They wanted to be first. James and John were not only members of the twelve, they belonged to an even more select group of three. Several times in the Gospels we read that James, John and Peter were with Jesus during some peak moment—on the Mount of Transfiguration, for example. But now James and John were trying to nose out Peter and reduce the select trio to a twosome. And their strategy was to have their mother go to Jesus to "sew it up." Before Peter could say a word, before he could launch a counterattack, they would be assured of their deserved greatness.

What a brilliant plan! What marvelous strategy! Of course, they would leave it up to Jesus to determine who would sit on his right and who would sit on his left. Inwardly, both James and John seemed to think they deserved the place of greatest honor—on his right. But they were brothers and determined to "hang together." One of them would be in first place with the other running a close second.

That spirit of "first place" and "greatness" finds its way into the church so often. Early in my ministry, I worked as an Associate in several Billy Graham Crusades. As I was closely involved with leading pastors and Christian businessmen, I was astonished and disappointed at the maneuvering and jockeying for position that went on. So often they would hang back and do nothing until Mr. Graham arrived in the city for the actual crusade services. Then they would come out of the woodwork.

Every one of them wanted to be close to Mr. Graham. They would vie for "first place" or the "best place" at luncheon tables or on the crusade platform. Each wanted to be the greatest—to be in first place.

By contrast, the majority of pastors and Christian lay leaders served quietly and effectively during the months of preparation for the crusade. They didn't think of greatness, and weren't concerned about who would gain recognition or who would be in first place. They simply served the Lord and others as true servant leaders.

3. *We must follow the example of Jesus.* He provided practical examples for his teaching. He was the supreme example of how servant leaders should operate. Imagine, the Lord of the universe came to earth as a servant! He came to serve. And he came not only to serve, but to give his life as a ransom for many

(Matthew 20:28). While other leaders take, Jesus gives. While other leaders have slaves and servants waiting upon them hand and foot, responding to their every desire, Jesus serves.

What an example Jesus has given us. What a powerful statement about Christian leadership. And what a model for us to follow and to imitate. Two basic elements of servant leadership are revealed in the teaching of Jesus in Matthew 20:28. If we are to be effective as servant leaders, we must implement them in two ways.

A. *Serving:* Serving is central; it is imperative. God has called us to serve—to minister to the authentic needs of people with the love of Jesus Christ and in the power of the Holy Spirit.

How do we serve? As Jesus did. He is the perfect example of a servant. This is seen clearly in the Gospels. And in Paul's letters we read that he humbled himself; he made himself nothing, taking upon himself the very nature or form of a servant (Philippians 2:7–8). Jesus didn't merely "act" like a servant. He became a servant!

B. *Giving:* Jesus said that he came to "give" his life a ransom for many. As servant leaders we must be willing to give of ourselves to others. In fact, we must be willing to give our very lives for others. John, the beloved disciple, expressed it in this way, "This is how we know what love is: Jesus Christ laid down his life for us. And we ought to lay down our lives for our brothers" (1 John 3:16).

John then proceeds to share a practical example

of how this "giving" should take place. "If anyone has material possessions and sees his brother in need but has no pity on him, how can the love of God be in him?" He concludes his teaching by declaring, "Dear children, let us not love with words or tongue but with actions and in truth" (vss. 17–18).

The implications are clear. The servant leader must be ready to give to others whatever God has given to him or her. The servant leader owns nothing; all he or she has comes from the Lord and is readily available to be given to anyone who needs it.

Professor Robert Saucy understood this principle well when he said, "Some talk of a new style of leadership today as involving servanthood. More collegial, less domineering. Yet there is still a radical difference. This alternate leadership is used as a strategy to lead to gain the goal of the leader which is the good of the business or himself. Jesus is not talking about taking the role of a servant or a servant leadership style. He is talking about being a servant. The radical difference is that the servant leads totally for the good of other people. The people he leads are his ultimate goal, they are not means to another end."[6]

Jesus taught this principle clearly when he said, "Give to everyone who asks you, and if anyone takes what belongs to you, do not demand it back. Do to others as you would have them do to you" (Luke 6:30–31). Servant leaders are generous givers—even as their Lord gives and gives—and gives again!

CHAPTER 6

SERVANT LEADERSHIP:
A Working Model

God wants us to be examples to others. But in order for us to be examples to the "flock," we must be following the Chief Shepherd as the Lord of our lives. We must be allowing the Holy Spirit to fill us with the fruit of the Spirit and to endow us with the gifts of the Spirit which he chooses to entrust to us. We must serve the Lord and his flock willingly and eagerly and be examples who reflect the character of Jesus Christ our Lord.

Be shepherds of God's flock that is under your
care, serving as overseers—not because you
must, but because you are willing as God
wants you to be; not greedy for money, but eager
to serve; not lording it over those entrusted to you,
but being examples to the flock.
—1 Peter 5:2–3

OVER AND OVER AGAIN I HAVE EMPHASIZED THE TRUTH that Jesus is our perfect model of servant leadership. He is our example; we are to follow him. But, how do we pull it off? How can we follow the example of Jesus? Where is a working model that I can both understand and follow?

Peter responds to our questions in his first Epistle with great sensitivity and appropriateness. As you will remember, he once faced the very dilemma which we face—servant leadership was as unnatural to him as it is to us. Of course, he had some advantages which we do not have. For example, he personally observed that servant leadership model of Jesus in action for some three years. Jesus was a vivid example to Peter day after day, as they lived and ministered together.

Several years later, when Peter had become one of the most influential leaders of the early Christian Church, he wrote some very important words about servant leadership. He wrote out of his own experience. And although he was an apostle and one of the most powerful and influential leaders in the church, he appealed to the other leaders as "fellow elders" (1 Peter 5:1). He did not write from a place of ecclesiastical hierarchy or political power. Instead, he wrote to others as a humble, loving servant of Jesus Christ— as a servant leader!

Shepherd God's Flock

Peter's first word of instruction to Christian leaders is that we should shepherd the flock of God entrusted to our care (1 Peter 5:2). The term "shepherd" is frequently used synonymously with that of "pastor." Peter's original readers were quite familiar with the word picture he was shaping here.

In the late twentieth century, we pick up on this imagery as a metaphor pointing to the servant leader who also has a great deal to do with shepherding. The entire concept of serving as a leader in Christ's kingdom relates to *people* more than tasks. Whatever the ministry that God has entrusted to us, we need to "shepherd the people" whom God is calling us to lead.

At the same time, we are to remember that it is "God's flock" and not ours. They are his people, the sheep of his pasture! We are simply the "under-shepherds" or the "under-leaders." Jesus Christ is the "Chief Shepherd" (v. 4). But as "under-shepherds," we carry a tremendous responsibility. We are accountable to God for how we lead and nurture those entrusted to our care.

James reminds us of the awesome responsibility when he writes, "Not many of you should presume to be teachers, my brothers, because you know that we who teach will be judged more strictly" (James 3:1). Indeed, we need to be careful how we feed and how we lead the flock of God! We are accountable to God—the Chief Shepherd—for how we do.

SERVE WILLINGLY

In Peter's instructions he addresses three major areas of concern that provide a practical working model for us. The first is that we should serve "Not because you must, but because you are willing as God wants you to be" (v. 2).

As I mentioned earlier, God is not concerned merely with "what" we do, he is concerned about "why" we do it. Without a doubt, love should be the basic motive for everything we do as Christians including leading others—and Peter seems to assume that as he goes on to discuss the motive of willingness. God wants us to serve him willingly.

There are always those in the church who emphasize the "oughtness" of service or leadership. They tend to be moralizers who live under the heavy cloak of legalism. Their motive seems to be duty. There is no joy in their service.

From a philosophical point of view, we would see these people as subscribing to determinism. Within such thinking, the human will does not have any place with Christian leadership. He or she does not will to do something, nor do they will not to do it. They have no choice in the matter. They simply do it because God has determined that they do so.

Peter would refute strongly that fatalistic approach. He calls upon us to escape from the mentality of serving God because we "have to." We should never lead simply out of a sense of obligation or because we have been "trapped" with no voice in the matter.

He seems to be saying that we should not fall into the trap of serving with a fatalistic spirit. Instead, we should serve willingly. That is how God desires for us to serve—willingly, from a heart filled with love and devotion.

SERVE EAGERLY

Next, we learn from Peter's words that God wants us to serve with eagerness. This is a paradox. After all, not many people are eager to be servants. In my twenty-five years in the ministry, not a single person has come to me to volunteer *eagerly* to be a servant. In fact, I have never had a person do that even without eagerness. Again we must say, it is contrary to human nature for any of us to be willing to be a servant. And it is even more contrary to be eager about it.

Before talking about eagerness, Peter discusses a more natural motive for people to be involved in leadership. That is "personal gain." Although several translations of the Bible would use the phrase, "not greedy for money," I believe that a more accurate translation from the original text is "not for personal gain."

Most of us who are in Christian leadership roles would be able to honestly admit with absolute integrity that we did not become involved in ministry because of the money we would make. Nearly all of us involved in vocational ministry could be making substantially more money if we entered another profession. It is true that there have been "con men" in the ministry who have been dishonest in their financial dealings and have taken advantage of people financially. But those people are in the distinct minority. Most people do not become involved in the ministry for the purpose of gaining personal wealth.

However, when we begin to discuss "personal gain," we are getting closer to home in most of our lives. This is a matter which is a temptation to most of us in leadership roles. It is a natural temptation for us to use our roles for self-advancement or for developing personal power. A true servant leader must run from every one of the temptations which would lead us to personal gain—whether it be money or power or prestige. God has called us to be servants; to shepherd his flock. And we should do so without regard for personal recognition or gain.

Let me ask you a personal question. "Why are you involved in the ministry?" Are you doing it willingly or do you feel that you are trapped without options? I believe that before we proceed with the reading of another word of this book, we should bow humbly before the Lord in prayer and ask him to reveal our true motives to us. And, if we are serving for the wrong motive, we should not continue to do so. We can ask God to forgive us, repent and begin to serve willingly as God would have us to do.

Robert Greenleaf spoke directly to this issue in

his book, *Servant Leadership*, "The servant-leader is a servant first. . . . It begins with the natural feeling that one wants to serve, to serve *first*. Then conscious choice brings one to aspire to lead. That person is sharply different from one who is *leader* first, perhaps because of the need to assuage an unusual power drive or to acquire material possessions. For such it will be a later choice to serve—after leadership is established. The leader-first and the servant-first are two extreme types. Between them there are shadings and blends that are part of the infinite variety of human nature.

"The difference manifests itself in the care taken by the servant-first to make sure that other people's highest priority needs are being served. The best test, and difficult to administer, is: Do those served grow as persons? Do they, *while being served*, become healthier, wiser, freer, more autonomous, more likely themselves to become servants?"[7]

In an article in *Pastoral Psychology*, Clyde Reid wrote specifically about the role of the minister as servant leader. ". . . the minister's task may be seen as an effort to free his people from dependence and help them to discover their mutual ministry. The minister as we know him today must lose his life as the absolute leader, the one who stands at the center of all activity, head and shoulders above the congregation—in order to find his true life as servant, as the releaser of the ministry of his people. This is an exciting and demanding concept of ministry."[8]

When that question has been settled with God,

we need to face a second question which is, "How do I serve in ministry?" Do I serve with personal gain in mind or do I serve eagerly? Again I would suggest that we pause for a time to allow the Lord to search our hearts in this matter. Let us repent if we need to repent, and let us determine to serve the Lord and others with eagerness.

When leaders are eager, the followers usually reflect that eagerness. I have noticed this to be true in local churches. Under normal conditions, a church family reflects the attitude and ministry style of its pastor. When a pastor is loving, the flock usually reflects a loving spirit. And when a pastor is eager, the people of God tend to be eager. Of course, the same principle operates in families.

For example, a number of years ago I had the privilege of becoming the personal friend of an internationally recognized Old Testament scholar. He was a brilliant man. Beyond that, he was a man who expressed great love and eagerness wherever he went. I observed two special things about his influence. First, his love and eagerness had a great effect upon his wife and children. They reflected those qualities in most authentic and personal ways. Secondly, wherever this man went, he had measurable influence. I observed him as he ministered in academic circles, public gatherings, church services and even small groups. His influence was always unmistakable. His eagerness was contagious.

I believe that God desires every one of us who are servant leaders to serve with eagerness, regardless of our specific roles. The Lord desires parents, pastors, administrators, corporate presidents and university provosts—Christian leaders in every arena of leadership—to serve him and others with eagerness.

SERVE AS EXAMPLES

Peter now moves on with his instructions as he tells us that we are to serve as examples to God's people. Again, Peter seems to be going against the normal way of leading people. Most leaders tend to lead by asserting their authority. Jesus had earlier pointed out that the Gentiles' style of leading people was to "lord it over them" and "exercise authority over them" (Matthew 20:25).

But as leaders in whatever capacity we serve, we are not to throw our weight around. A pastor, Sunday school teacher, or committee chairman is not to be a dictator. That was not Jesus' style.

Pei-Lu Liu, a wonderful Chinese Christian friend, recently shared a vivid illustration with me concerning the importance of being an example. In a letter to me, she wrote, "Lately I have been meditating on servanthood. When I think of servanthood, I think of light. In ancient China, outdoor lightings were provided by lanterns. Whenever a guest came to visit at night, it was always the servant who carried the lantern and led the way so that the guest might follow and see the path."[9]

The same principle is true in our family life. Many Christian husbands mistakenly believe that God has called them to be the dictators in their homes. They treat wife and children as objects who should respond to their every whim. Christian husbands and fathers are not called to be dictators but to be servant leaders; they are not to "use" family members but to serve them and to build them up to become more and more like Christ himself. That is what Mary Alvarez discovered and so must all of us who have the privilege of being parents.

In his book, *The Church*, Hans Küng has stated this truth well. "Authority in the community is derived not from the holding of a certain rank, not from a special tradition, not from old age or long membership in the community but from the performance of a ministry in the Spirit. The obedience of all is due to God, Christ, the Spirit; only a limited, and never a unilateral obedience is due to other men in the community. The consequence of the obedience of all to God, Christ and the Spirit is voluntary and *mutual* submission, the voluntary ministry of all to all, voluntary obedience to the different charisms of others."[10]

God wants us to be examples to others. But to be examples to the "flock," we must be following the Chief Shepherd as the Lord of our lives. We must be allowing the Holy Spirit to fill us with the fruit of the Spirit and to endow us with the gifts of the Spirit which he chooses to entrust to us. We must serve the Lord and his flock willingly and eagerly and be examples who reflect the character of Jesus Christ our Lord.

CHAPTER 7

SERVANT LEADERSHIP:

Leading Like a Shepherd

Our greatest task is to help every person to follow Jesus as the Chief Shepherd. Our greatest desire should be for them to fix their eyes upon Jesus and to run the race set before them with great perseverance, looking unto Jesus, the author and finisher of the faith (Hebrews 12:1, 2). It is our joyous task to encourage and enable them to do that.

"I am the good shepherd. The good shepherd
lays down his life for the sheep. . . .
I am the good shepherd. I know my sheep
and my sheep know me."
—John 10:11, 14

JESUS REFERRED TO HIMSELF AS THE "GOOD SHEP-
herd." In the tenth chapter of the Gospel of John, he
explains what the good shepherd does, and he teaches
us what good shepherding is all about. To be an
effective servant leader, I believe that we need to
know the Good Shepherd and become related to him
personally. Then we need to practice the principles of
good shepherding which he alone can teach us.

THE SHEPHERD KNOWS THE SHEEP

Jesus said that one of the qualities of an effective
shepherd is this: he knows his sheep. In the world in
which Jesus lived and ministered, shepherds had
a very personal relationship with their sheep. The
flocks were usually small. The shepherd was intimately involved in the life of each of his sheep from
the time it was born. He cared for every need of
his sheep, making certain that they had adequate
food and water, seeing that they didn't stray or get

lost, and protecting them from every potential enemy.

To be an effective servant leader, we need to know the people entrusted to our care. At first thought, this sounds simple. However, I am convinced that it is a major challenge for most of us. Let me share the challenge from my own perspective as one who is committed to being an effective servant leader of several groups of people whom God has entrusted to my care.

First, there is the wonderful congregation that I serve as a senior pastor. Since there are several thousands of members plus scores of visitors each month, it is virtually impossible for me to know each individual personally. However, even though I cannot know each person intimately, I am still responsible for them and to the Chief Shepherd to make certain that at least one of the other pastors from our church staff knows each person whom I cannot know. It is imperative that every person in the congregation is known personally by at least one of the pastors.

Second, I am a husband and a father. I love my wife and our three children very much. It seems it would be very simple for me to know each of them very well. But it isn't. I need to keep working at it. Our lives are very busy. As my children have grown older, they are active with schoolwork, church activities and work assignments along with personal and social engagements.

We find that we need to plan specific times with each other so that we do not "lose touch." I want not only to know *who* my wife and children are, I want to know *where* they are in life, where they are growing, what needs they are facing, and how they are feeling. I want to know them well—in the present tense! Only then can I effectively care for them as the Lord would want me to do.

Third, I teach classes periodically in a theological seminary and frequently lead seminars for pastors. During that brief period of class or seminar time, I believe I have at least a temporary shepherd's responsibility. I need to become acquainted with my students. I do not want to treat them as though they were mere objects; I want to get to know each class member as a unique and special person.

Finally, I have the joy of leading a wonderful pastoral team and church staff. Again, I long to know each of those brothers and sisters personally. I believe God has entrusted a special pastoral responsibility to me to care for the pastors along with some of the key lay leaders of the church. I am in the process of learning how I can most effectively be their shepherd and servant leader.

These are the key shepherding and servant leadership assignments that God has entrusted to me during this period of my life. Most of you also have a multiple list of persons whom the Lord is calling you to serve and shepherd. You are also called to relate to some of the people in your life as a servant leader. Most of us have at least one shepherding responsibility which God is entrusting to us. Each of those shepherding activities includes servant leadership. In fact, all of our interpersonal relationships require the spirit of a servant whether leadership is involved or not.

If we are to be effective as servant leaders, it is imperative that we know the sheep—that is the people whom the Lord has entrusted to our care. Jesus proceeds to tell us that a good shepherd calls his or her own sheep by name. Recently I read that the average American knows only 100 to 150 people by name. Few people can remember more faces or names than that.

Most of us have difficulty remembering names. But a good shepherd loves people enough to work at learning the names of the persons who are entrusted to his or her care. People are touched deeply when we remember them by name. It has a measurable effect upon most persons. I find that I best remember names when I get to know someone by finding out specific details of that person's life such as where he or she works and lives—or what people enjoy doing. Repeating a person's name every time I see him or her also helps me to remember well. An effective servant leader knows the people whom he or she is leading and calls them by name.

THE SHEEP KNOW THE SHEPHERD

Not only does the good shepherd know his or her own sheep, the sheep know their shepherd. Jesus said that the sheep listen to his voice (John 10:3). He goes on to say that because they know his voice, they follow him. In other words, they trust him because they know him (v. 5). At the same time, they will never follow a stranger. In fact, they will run away from him because they do not recognize a stranger's voice (v. 5).

This teaching of Jesus has vitally important implications for those of us who would be servant leaders. It focuses upon interpersonal relationships in which we know the persons whom we lead, and they know us. Implied in all of this is that we love the sheep personally and individually. We have to conduct ourselves so they want to know us. We need to build authentic trust so that they will follow us through thick and thin as we follow Christ.

Love is usually immediate when we meet other Christians. However, trust must be earned. Trust takes time to develop. It requires a relationship of mutual involvement. People do not follow us merely because we have been assigned to be leaders. We need to earn the right to lead others and to be trusted. As Christian servant leaders, our lives need to be expressing the love and grace of Jesus Christ—and the fruit of the Spirit. As I have said earlier, we should expect people to follow us only as we follow Jesus.

In fact, I believe that for those of us who are servant leaders, the trust which we earn over a period of time is wonderfully combined with a level of trust which God gives to Christians as they follow Jesus and as they are sensitive to the leading of the Holy Spirit in their lives. The weaving of those two strands of trust result in great blessing to us as servant leaders, to the sheep themselves and to the Chief Shepherd.

LAYING DOWN OUR LIVES

The good shepherd knows his sheep, calls them by name, loves them, and earns their trust. But he does much more than that. The good shepherd literally lays down his life for the sheep. Jesus did that! He said, "The reason the Father loves me is that I lay down my life—only to take it up again. No one takes it from me, but I lay it down of my own accord" (John 10:17–18). Of course, that is exactly what Jesus accomplished when he died on the cross and shed his blood for the remission of our sins. He gave his life for the sheep so that they could have life eternal (John 3:16). We rejoice and give thanks for this wonderful act of salvation which relates personally to everyone of us.

I believe that this teaching of Jesus carries some personal implications for each of us who has been called of God to be a servant leader. We can never lay down our lives as the atonement for the sins of others as Jesus did. But we may be called upon to lay down our lives for the sheep in other specific ways. Many of the Christian martyrs down through the history of the church have done so. Few of us will be called to do so—but I believe that we must be willing to give our lives for others. The one who truly loves others will be willing to sacrifice for them—even with his or her life!

At least, we are called to give our lives for the sheep in little ways day by day such as being available to them when they authentically need us. Being inconvenienced is another one of the realities of being a servant leader. Jesus reminds of this fact in his parable of the lost sheep (Luke 15). Ninety-nine of the sheep were responsible and obedient enough to be where they were supposed to be—safely in the sheep-fold for the night. But one of the little guys was lost.

The shepherd probably had a dinner engagement that night or perhaps there was a Monday night football game on television. In any event, the shepherd loved the little lost sheep so much that he went out looking for him at night. It was not convenient; it was not comfortable; it was not desirable—but he did it because he cared about the sheep. He was willing to be inconvenienced and even to risk his life for the one little lost sheep.

Servant leaders learn quickly that there are many risks and scores of inconveniences in shepherding and caring for persons. Over the years, I have noticed that so many of the problems encountered by people take place either at meal time or in the middle of the night. And hurting people often feel the most lonely or the most lost at times of special holidays such as Christmas or Thanksgiving. Sensitive shepherds learn to anticipate those times of special need. They may plan strategic ministries for those occasions such as inviting hurting sheep for Thanksgiving dinner or for a Christmas celebration. A servant leader is sensitive to the needs of his sheep and is always on call.

A GOOD SHEPHERD LEADS

A good shepherd leads his sheep. In one sense, this statement is so obvious that we might feel it goes without saying. However, in the reality of life, it is vitally important that we understand this principle. Jesus stated, "He . . . leads them out. When he has brought out all his own, he goes on ahead of them" (John 10:3–4).

Many so-called leaders believe that because they have been given a specific responsibility of leadership, people will follow them automatically. Most of us have learned (some of us in difficult, painful ways) that such an assumption is not always valid. True, there are some good people who will follow anyone who is designated as leader. But others will not. Just this week, for example, I counseled with a hurting pastor who faced a leadership problem similar to that faced by Harry Gladstone.

Just one year ago this man was called to be the senior pastor of a large mainline denominational church. His predecessor had served as pastor for some four decades. All the people had loved and followed the former pastor. He knew, loved and cared for them over the years. But many of those same persons were not ready to follow a new pastor whom they did not know very well and did not yet trust.

The Board of Elders of the church tried to legislate trust upon the membership. They told the people that they must trust the new pastor if he was to lead them effectively. Of course, that strategy did not work. It built more walls than bridges. The new pastor is having to pay the price of earning the trust of the people. By taking the initiative, he is getting to know and love them. This will require time and patience and specific acts of serving. Only when he has wept with hurting people and has helped mend broken relationships and has brought comfort to the mourning families will he earn their trust.

As we have seen, Jesus wisely tells us that the good shepherd knows his sheep, calls them by name and then "leads them out!" What an important leadership principle for a servant leader to understand. Effective leadership demands that we go out ahead of the sheep. We do not merely "tell" the sheep where to go; we "show" them by moving out in front of them and then by "leading" them. The true servant leader does not send the sheep over the next hill on their own. He goes on ahead of them to be certain that everything is all right. He "leads" them! This is one of the ways in which people learn to trust the servant leader. Words of comfort and encouragement are important, but they are not enough.

The people of God want to see where their servant leader is. They desire the security and comfort of his presence. They long for his rod and staff to protect them from the enemies that may be lurking around the next corner or over the next hill. The effective servant leader is highly visible in his leading and caring and comforting. He follows the example of Jesus Christ.

THERE SHALL BE ONE FLOCK

A final principle that Jesus shared in this teaching is found in verse 16, "I have other sheep that are not of this sheep pen. I must bring them also. They too will listen to my voice, and there shall be one flock and one shepherd."

Human shepherds tend to divide their flock and to separate their flock from other flocks. That is fully understandable—with both sheep and with people. Jesus acknowledged this when he said that sheep know only the voice of their own shepherd; they will follow only him.

But in the kingdom of God, things are different. In his kingdom, there is only one Chief Shepherd, and he is Jesus Christ! However, God appoints "undershepherds" to care for portions of his flock. I am an undershepherd, and so are many of you. One of the first principles that an undershepherd must understand is that within the kingdom of God, there is only one flock. "There is neither Jew nor Greek, slave nor free, male nor female, for you are all one in Christ Jesus" (Galatians 3:28).

One of the temptations which we face as leaders is to build our own personal kingdom; to control our own loyal following; to look upon the flock that God has entrusted to our care as our own. We develop a vocabulary that includes such possessive phrases as "my congregation" or "my people." Such leaders often try to separate "their flock" from other people in God's larger flock with such overt excuses as desiring to protect them from impure doctrine. These same leaders frequently develop the "we—they" or "in—out" syndromes. They contend that they alone are the pure and righteous. Everyone else should be looked upon as impure and unrighteous at worst or should be held as highly suspect at best.

Servant leaders must not lead in that way. We must realize that we are first servants of Jesus Christ and accountable to him. Jesus died for all the people of the world. He invites people to enter his flock. We often tend to keep them out by our own criteria. Jesus openly declares, "Whoever will may come!" We are privileged to be entrusted with the care of some of the people of God—and they *are* his people.

Our greatest task is to help every person to follow Jesus as the Chief Shepherd. Our greatest desire should be for them to fix their eyes upon Jesus and to run the race set before them with great perseverance, looking unto Jesus, the author and finisher of the faith (Hebrews 12:1, 2). It is our joyous task to encourage and enable them to do that.

Servant leaders are always builders of lives. They are constantly encouraging and enabling the "followers" to grow in the grace and knowledge of Jesus Christ. They never develop their own disciples; they give themselves to the task of developing disciples of Jesus. They minister with the deep conviction that there is one shepherd and one flock. Jesus Christ is that good shepherd, and the flock is his!

CHAPTER 8

SERVANT LEADERSHIP:

A Warning to Bad Leaders

Servant leaders are accountable to God ultimately. And he will hold us accountable for how we lead and care for his people!

This is what the Sovereign Lord says: Woe to the
shepherds of Israel who only take care of
themselves! Should not shepherds
take care of the flock?
—Ezekiel 34:2

WHAT HAPPENS WHEN A SERVANT LEADER FAILS TO lead? Or what is the result of a Harry Gladstone becoming so tired and discouraged that he resigns his pastorate and leaves the ministry? Or what takes place when a Christian executive like John Steelman fails with his leadership style or when a Mary Alvarez rules her children like an angry dictator rather than as a loving servant leader? Or what happens when scores of Christian leaders choose to lead with styles other than that of a loving, caring shepherd?

Does it matter to God? Or does it matter to us? The answer should be a loud and emphatic *"Yes!!"* It does matter! God cares when people are neglected and abused. God cares when his leaders become selfish or corrupted with money or power. God grieves when his leaders become dictators—when they rule like the "Gentiles." He is touched with the cries of his people when they become sheep without a shepherd. He longs for his servant leaders to love and care for his sheep.

Centuries ago, God expressed this deep concern through a prophecy that he gave to the prophet Ezekiel. That prophetic word contains a powerful and relevant message for all of us who have been called to be servant leaders. Let us explore several salient points from this powerful passage found in Ezekiel 34.

1. *Woe to the shepherds who take care of only themselves (Ezekiel 34:2)!* This message bears a great resemblance to that of Peter when he warns servant leaders about tending the flock of God only for personal gain. God has not called us to the primary ministry of taking care of ourselves. Instead, he has entrusted some of his precious people to our care. They are his people—the sheep of his pasture.

Ezekiel wrote about shepherds of the Lord who had taken wonderful care of themselves. "They had eaten the curds of the sheep's milk, had clothed themselves with the wool of the sheep and had slaughtered the best of the sheep for their own nourishment" (v. 3). In other words, they had "used" the sheep for their own benefit. They did not care about giving; only about receiving. They had become totally selfish in their role as shepherds. They exploited the people and gained personal benefits from their shepherding, but they gave nothing in return.

It is natural to care for ourselves. Putting ourselves first is one of the basic expressions of sin. But that was not the only sin which God addressed to those shepherds through his prophetic message. Another major sin was strongly implied—the fact that these shepherds had been taking care of "only" themselves. By so doing, they had been totally neglecting the needs of their sheep. They had not been providing for the persons whom the Lord had put under their care.

They had not merely been doing a sloppy job of caring for their sheep. They were not taking care of them at all. They turned their backs on the people for whom they were responsible—and on the ministry of service to which God had called them.

Evidently, they thought that God wouldn't notice. They had been deceived by their sin. They had become so totally absorbed in "doing their own thing" and "caring for themselves" that they had not only completely forgotten their sheep, they had also forgotten their God.

But he had not forgotten them—nor had he forgotten their responsibility to him and to his sheep as his shepherds. The day of reckoning had come.

2. *You have not strengthened the weak (v. 4)!* The Lord proceeded to point out some of the specific failures of his shepherds. First, he accused them of not strengthening the weak. Every flock seems to have at least some members who are weak. They require special care and attention.

Every servant leader realizes that he or she will never lead a group of people who are totally strong. The weak are always with us. In fact, I am reminded of several dear people who represent the weak of our church family. Several of them require personal time from me every week. A few of them require some time every day from a pastor. My dear wife Jeannie cares for some of them each day. A good and faithful servant leader does not ignore the weak persons in his or her care. Servant leaders love and care for the weak!

3. *You have not healed the sick (v. 4)!* Healing is a ministry which we normally assign to doctors and hospitals within our society. However, it appears to me that we have the responsibility to care for the healing needs of those we are called to lead. James shared this basic message with us, "Is any one of you sick? He should call the elders of the church to pray over him and anoint him with oil in the name of the Lord. And the prayer offered in faith will make the sick person well; the Lord will raise him up" (James 5:14–15).

The Lord is the source of all healing. Neither of these passages suggests that we should not go to doctors or take medicine or have surgery. However, the Scriptures do teach us that the servant leader has been entrusted with a healing ministry. It is always right for us to pray for the sick—and then leave the results to God. Whenever any members of my congregation become ill, I urge them to visit the doctor, and I also suggest they ask the elders of the church to anoint them with oil and pray for them.

Then, too, even as we are to be involved with physical healing, we are not to neglect the healing of memories and emotions. People are a wonderful blend of physical, emotional, mental and spiritual beings. God's healing power is available for every area of our lives.

4. *You have not bound up the injured (v. 4)!*
The Lord scolded the shepherds for not binding up
the sheep that had been injured. That word reminds
me so much of the parable of Jesus concerning the
Good Samaritan (Luke 10:25–37). The priest who
passed by did not stop to help the injured man nor did
the Levite. Both were religious leaders. Both should
have been servant leaders for the Lord.

But neither of them stopped to bind up the
wounds of the injured man. Perhaps they felt they
were too busy. Or maybe they were frightened at the
prospect of being beaten and robbed themselves. Or
there may have been another reason for their failure
to help—the very reason which God shared through
the prophet Ezekiel. Maybe they were so preoccu-
pied with themselves and their own self-fulfilling
religious duties that they simply ignored those who
were hurting; their agenda for the day simply did not
include an injured, hurting person.

What a warning that should be to us as servant
leaders. We need to be like the Good Samaritan
whose only apparent agenda appeared to be to respond to the needs of an injured man. He took pity
upon him, went to him, and bandaged his wounds,
pouring on oil and wine. He took personal risk and
was inconvenienced and took time and ministered
to the man. He put the man on his own donkey,
transported him to an inn and took care of him. And
the next day, he gave the innkeeper enough money
to care for the injured man until he was well (v.
33–35).

What a message there is in that parable for all us who aspire to be servant leaders! As you will remember, Jesus told the parable to illustrate one of his most central teachings, "Love the Lord your God with all your heart and with all your soul and with all your strength and with all your mind, and love your neighbor as yourself" (v. 27). That teaching should be the very foundation of our Christian lifestyle and the very heart of servant leadership.

5. *You have not brought back the strays (v. 4)!* Good shepherds watch over their flocks carefully and faithfully. There are not many sheep that are allowed to stray. The very fact that there are strays is somewhat of an indictment on the shepherd. Good shepherds know their sheep by name and their sheep recognize the voice of their shepherd and stay close to him or her.

Good shepherds go out ahead of their sheep to make certain that everything is safe. They don't lead their sheep into areas where they can stray easily. But even the best of shepherds sometimes fails and allows one or two sheep to stray. But such shepherds don't merely admit their mistake. They do something about it. They go out and bring in the strays.

In our leadership roles, it is important for us to have the same concern for members of the flock that have strayed. I once had a very painful experience with some of the elders of a church I was pastoring. They were loving and kind men. But like most Americans, they were also expedient. They decided that they wanted to "clean up" our church membership roll by dropping the name of every member whom they couldn't locate.

I was deeply troubled at the very thought of such an approach. Instead, we organized a ministry that focused on attempting to find the strays—to go out after them with the love and compassion and patience of the Good Shepherd. Of course, once we located the strays, we attempted to minister to their needs. If God had led them to another flock, then we could joyfully release them. But even that could be done only after we had found them and loved them and cared for them.

6. *You have not searched for the lost (v. 4)!* Before his ascension, Jesus gave to us what is often called the "Great Commission." He instructed us to go into all the world and make disciples of all people.

At the very heart of that commission is the deep concern that God has for lost people. Jesus Christ said that rescuing the lost was his primary purpose for coming to earth. He came to "seek and to save those who were lost"!

Jesus shared a touching parable about a lost sheep (Luke 15:3–7). Although he spoke in parabolic form, there is little doubt that he was speaking about himself. He told the story of the shepherd who had one hundred sheep. Ninety-nine of them were safe in his care but one was lost. That shepherd left the ninety-nine in the safety of the open country while he searched for the one lost sheep.

And when he found it, he joyfully put it on his shoulders and took it home. Then he called his friends together for a celebration and said, "Rejoice with me; I have found my lost sheep" (v. 6). This message is the good news of salvation. Jesus has come to find the lost and to rescue them and to give them eternal life.

God's deep concern for the lost is also reflected in the prophecy of Ezekiel. He longs for his shepherds to "search for the lost." We cannot take a neutral attitude about the lost nor can we merely look for them passively. God wants us to "go out of our way" and "search" for those who are lost. And, according to the parable of Jesus, when we have found them, we need to bring them back to the fold with real rejoicing. There is great rejoicing in heaven over one sinner who repents, and there needs to be great joy in the heart of the servant leader and of all of the family or congregation when a lost member of the flock is found and returned to the fold.

7. *You have ruled them harshly and brutally (v. 4)!* The shepherds had not only neglected the sheep by not strengthening the weak, healing the sick, binding up the injured, and failing to bring back the strays and searching for the lost, they had also been guilty of ruling them harshly and brutalizing them. How tragic!

Most of us recoil at the very thought of such treatment of sheep or any other animal. But we are even more justifiably troubled by the thought of "person abuse." We live in a day when the sins of child, wife, and even husband abuse are communicated to us regularly in the newspaper and on radio and television. What a tragic indictment those sins are upon our society.

But God was actually accusing his shepherds of being guilty of this horrible sin, of abusing his sheep. First, they were treating them harshly. Those of us who are parents need to guard against this sin. Christian parents who are servant leaders must treat their children with love, respect, tenderness and gentleness—as Jesus would do!

The apostle Paul warns Christian fathers not to "provoke" or "exasperate" their children (Ephesians 6:4). Instead, we should bring our children up in the nurture and instruction of the Lord. In other words, we should treat our children just as the Lord would treat them. In fact, it is important for Christian parents to recognize that we are only the "underparents" or "undershepherds" of our children. If we are serious about following Jesus as Lord, we have given our children to Christ along with everything else we have in our possession. It is both awesome and freeing to know that we are caring for the Lord's children.

Of course, that realization is helpful to us as we contemplate our role as servant leaders. We care for the "Lord's people." They are never our own. We are merely overseers who are tending the flock of God entrusted to our care.

Secondly, these shepherds were guilty of treating their sheep brutally. It is one thing to be harsh. We normally think of that as verbal and emotional abuse. But when we speak of brutality, we are thinking of actual physical abuse. Can you imagine a shepherd of God's flock abusing the sheep in any way—emotionally, spiritually, physically or even sexually? It should not be so!

8. *You have scattered the flock (v. 5–6)!* Next, the Lord accused his shepherds of being responsible for scattering his flock. "So they were scattered because there was no shepherd, and when they were scattered they became food for all the wild animals" (v. 5).

That is what happens when a servant leader forsakes his flock. The people first scatter. They do not know what to do nor where to go. The biblical description of these hurting and disoriented people is intensely graphic—they are like sheep "without a shepherd." In my opinion, that is the ultimate description of lostness and helplessness. And it is the description of many people in our society—even in our churches—who need servant leaders to lead them.

9. *God is against such shepherds (v. 10)!* Can you think of anything more awesome and terrible than that—to have God against us? What a contrast this statement is to that of the apostle Paul when he declared, "If God is for us, who can be against us?" (Romans 8:31).

To state the matter bluntly, these shepherds had become traitors. They had "changed sides." They were no longer on God's side; they had moved to the side of sin by doing their own thing and going their own way. God was on one side, and they were on the other.

10. *God will hold such shepherds accountable for his flock (v. 10)!* Accountability is not a popular word in our world. Yet God still demands it of any who will be leaders in his kingdom. As we have seen, that is what James means when he contends that those of us who teach will be judged with greater strictness. Jesus' parable of the talents also documents this fact.

In the concluding remarks of his parable about the three servants to whom the talents were given, Jesus stated this truth in another way, "From everyone who has been given much, much will be demanded; and from the one who has been entrusted with much, much more will be asked" (Luke 12:48). God demands accountability from his servants. We must give an account of what we have done with what he has given to us—including the honored role of being a servant leader in his kingdom.

Paul taught this truth clearly to the Christians at Corinth when he wrote, "So then, men ought to regard us as servants of Christ and as those entrusted with the secret things of God. Now it is required that those who have been given a trust must prove faithful" (1 Corinthians 4:1–2).

Years ago, I met a servant leader who chose these two verses as the major guiding principle of his life. He was one of the most successful stockbrokers in all of Canada. And he attributed his success to his faithfulness in obeying this basic teaching. He attempted to be a faithful steward of all that God entrusted to him. This stewardship even included the way in which he conducted the affairs of his clients. He realized that he was accountable to God for every resource and opportunity of life.

Servant leaders are accountable to God ultimately. And he will hold us accountable for how we lead and care for his people!

11. *I will remove them from tending the flock (v. 10)!* Finally, God said that he would remove such shepherds from tending his flock. Once again we are reminded of the basic fact that it is his flock, and he is in charge. If we fail to care adequately for the people of God, he will remove us.

That is an awesome statement. Many would ask, "How does God remove his leaders from tending his flock?" An initial reply would have to be, "That is God's business. He does it as he wishes to do it!"

However, most of us have lived long enough to observe the Lord in this awesome activity of removing leaders from roles which they have neglected and/or abused. Sometimes we have seen a bishop or district superintendent remove a pastor from an assigned ministry. Other times, we have seen a Christian executive lose his job or a Christian father lose his family. Several times, I have witnessed the ultimate removal of a leader—death.

Many may object to the very mention of such a possibility. But God is God! He cares for his sheep. He has promised to "rescue his sheep" and to "look after them" (v. 10–11). He will do so regardless of our failures or objections. He is the Good Shepherd who cares for his sheep.

CHAPTER 9

SERVANT LEADERSHIP:

Leaders and Followers

To be a true disciple of Jesus, we are told that we must deny ourselves, take up our cross and follow him (Mark 8:34). Of course, that demands a great deal of commitment and obedience. And, if we are to obey the Lord, we must become active participants of his body—the church! This requires that we become servants of Christ and servants of one another.

. . . they have devoted themselves to the
service of the saints. I urge you brothers
to submit to such as these and to
everyone who joins in the work, and labors at it
. . . . Such men deserve recognition.
—1 Corinthians 16:15–18

SOME CHRISTIANS ARE CALLED TO BE LEADERS; BUT all Christians are called to be followers. In fact, most of us are called to be both *leaders* and *followers.* To illustrate what I mean by those statements, let's return to our friends Harry, John and Mary.

As you will remember, Mary is a single parent. In that role, she is called to be a servant leader. But she fills other roles as well. For example, she is an active member of a local church. Within that community of faith, her primary role is to be a follower—a member of the congregation.

John is a young executive. As he functions in that role, he is called by God to serve within the role of a Christian servant leader. In his family situation, he is both a husband and a father and, therefore, seeks to fill both those roles as a servant leader. In his church, he is the chairperson of the Christian Education Committee. Again, he functions as a servant leader. But he also serves in several roles as a follower. As a member of the congregation he needs to follow the pastor and elders of the church. While at work, he reports to one of the vice-presidents of his company.

Even Harry, as a minister, has a role as a follower. It is true that he serves as the senior minister of a large church and, therefore, he is responsible to provide servant leadership to a large number of people. But he has the role of a follower as well. In Harry's particular denomination, he is accountable to the presbytery. In other denominations, a pastor might be accountable to a bishop or to a district superintendent. Above all, every pastor and Christian leader is responsible and accountable to God. All of us—even leaders—need to be accountable to others. All Christians are followers!

BEING AN EFFECTIVE FOLLOWER

If we had titled this book, "How to Be an Effective Servant Follower," probably not many copies would have been sold. In fact, my father would probably be the only one to buy a copy since my mother has already gone to heaven!

The point is clear; most people don't want to be followers; most of us want to be leaders! We want to be first. Furthermore, we live in a macho society where every person likes to do his or her own thing. We long to be captain of our ship, master of our own destiny. We call that kind of mentality an "independent spirit."

We tend to follow our own instincts, but Jesus

says that we must deny ourselves, take up our cross and follow him (Mark 8:34). We enjoy satisfying our appetites, but God tells us to beat our bodies into subjection so that we can serve him (1 Corinthians 9:27).

In my opinion, one of the true tests of our qualifications to be effective servant leaders is whether or not we are willing to become true servant followers. First, we follow Jesus Christ as Lord, and then we follow those whom God has designated as our human leaders.

The Word of God gives us our instructions for being good followers. For example, in the closing words of Paul's first letter to the Corinthian Church, he referred to the household of Stephanas who were the first converts in Achaia. He described those church leaders as people who "devoted themselves to the service of the saints" (16:15). In other words, Paul implies that they did not merely serve the saints passively. They served actively and were vivid examples of servant leaders.

Paul instructed the Corinthian believers to submit themselves to those leaders and to everyone who joins in the work (1 Corinthians 16:16). He then spoke about Stephanas, Fortunatus and Achaicus who had come to visit him with supplies. By doing so, they had greatly encouraged Paul and had refreshed his spirit. Paul concludes, "Such men deserve recognition" (1 Corinthians 16:17, 18).

Paul seems to be making it clear here that recognition is due those servant leaders in the church who have been called of God and have been anointed by the Holy Spirit. We are to recognize and accept their authority.

The author of the Book of Hebrews writes, "Remember your leaders, those who spoke the word of God to you. Consider the outcome of their way of life and imitate their faith" (13:7). This teaching, addressed specifically to "followers," parallels that of Paul written from a leader's perspective when he wrote, "Follow my example, as I follow the example of Christ" (1 Corinthians 11:1).

OBEY YOUR LEADERS

Next, the author of Hebrews presents some even more specific instructions. "Obey your leaders and submit to their authority. They keep watch over you as men who must give an account. Obey them so that their work will be a joy, not a burden, for that would be of no advantage to you" (Hebrews 13:17). This passage reveals several important principles of leading and following in the kingdom of God.

1. *Obey your leaders.* First there is the matter of obeying. Obedience is the key to Christian discipleship. Few committed Christians would deny that we are expected to obey God in all that we do. Jesus said, "If anyone loves me, he will obey my teaching. My Father will love him, and we will come to him and make our home with him. He who does not love me will not obey my teaching" (John 14:23, 24). John is saying here that when we obey Christ, he and the

Father actively abide in us in the person of the Holy Spirit. Jesus said, "But you know him, for he lives with you and will be in you" (v. 17).

Obedience to God releases the presence and the power of the Holy Spirit in our lives. As we have seen, along with the Holy Spirit comes the "fruit of the Spirit" including "love, joy, peace, patience, kindness, goodness, faithfulness, gentleness and self-control." All of these are wonderful fringe benefits of the life of obedience.

But we need to obey for other important reasons as well. We prove our love for Christ when we obey him. It is not enough that we merely tell him that we love him or even that we sing beautiful hymns expressing our love for him. The proof of our love for Christ is our obedience!

And that life of obedience also extends to the leaders whom God has placed in our lives. God tells us that we *should obey those leaders* as they point us toward the life of obeying Christ. It is not a matter of blindly obeying, but of obeying the Lord who called them to be our leaders in his kingdom.

2. *Submit to their authority.* Obedience is a great challenge for all of us. But the Word of God now proceeds to tell us that we should submit to the authority of these servant leaders. Within our society, we may "soften" the word obedience so that it becomes somewhat palatable. No one likes to submit! And no one likes authority!

God instructs us to submit to our leaders. This is more than the "mutual submission" we read about in

Ephesians 5. This is real, honest-to-goodness submission which takes place because these leaders have been given authority over us by God himself.

3. *They keep watch over you.* One of the functions of a good servant leader is to keep watch over those entrusted to his or her care. Like a good shepherd watching over his sheep, the servant leader keeps watch over the people of God.

For some of us, that is a comforting and encouraging statement. It is wonderful to know that we have pastors who care for us. When we are sick or lonely, or when we are facing a need, we can always call our pastor and know that he will care for us. There is always someone to whom we can go for help.

However, for others, the very idea that someone is watching over them is threatening. During the past eleven years of my ministry, I have served on the pastoral staff of two large churches, each with several thousand members. And during that time, I have discovered that some people attend larger churches primarily because they want to remain anonymous. They do not want to become involved or to be accountable to anyone.

For example, while on the pastoral staff of the First Presbyterian Church of Hollywood, I met a dear older lady after one of the morning worship services. She told me something which hurt me deeply. With a twinkle in her eyes she said, "I have been attending this church for some twenty-five years and you are the first pastor I have ever talked with." In other words, she had been avoiding the pastors for all those years.

She enjoyed being uninvolved and uncommitted to the body of Christ!

In a real sense, such persons do not want to obey anyone or to submit to any authority. Such people usually attempt to maintain that same kind of relationship with God. They foolishly attempt to receive all the "fringe benefits" of the church and of Christian discipleship without making any commitment. Unfortunately, they do not seem to realize that such a Christian lifestyle is not viable.

To be a true disciple of Jesus, we are told that we must deny ourselves, take up our cross and follow him (Mark 8:34). Of course, that demands a great deal of commitment and obedience. And, if we are to obey the Lord, we must become active participants in his body—the church. This requires that we become servants of Christ and servants of one another. Each of us uses our spiritual gifts to serve one another and to build one another up to Christian maturity.

4. *They must give an account.* All of us are accountable within God's family. As certainly as followers are accountable to obey their servant leaders and to submit to their authority, so are the servant leaders accountable to God for how they care for the persons entrusted to them. It is a great privilege to be a servant leader; it is also an awesome responsibility!

This teaching reminds us of the parable of the talents (Matthew 25). Jesus told of a master who gave one of his servants one talent, another servant two talents and another five talents. He assumed that each would invest his talents wisely. But when he returned from his business trip, he received only a mixed response. He was pleased to find that the servant with two talents had doubled his investment so that he was able to present the master with four talents. The servant with five talents had also doubled his investment. The delighted master said to both of those servants, "Well done, good and faithful servant! You have been faithful with a few things; I will put you in charge of many things. Come and share your master's happiness" (v. 23).

However, instead of investing his talent, the last servant buried it. To this lazy servant, his master replied ". . . take the talent from him and give it to the one who has the ten talents . . . . And throw that worthless servant outside, into the darkness, where there will be weeping and gnashing of teeth" (v. 26–30).

The truths of that parable relate strongly to the teaching of the Book of Hebrews. All servant leaders will someday appear before their Master to give an account of their stewardship of the lives of the people over whom they have given leadership. Servant leaders must give an account to God!

5. *Let their work be a joy.* The writer again appeals to the followers to obey their leaders "so that their work will be a joy" (Hebrews 13:17)! What practical and delightful teaching! It reminds me of some experiences I have had as a teenager with baby-sitting. Since I have always enjoyed children very much, some of those baby-sitting experiences were absolutely delightful. They were the occasions in

which the children were well behaved and obeyed my instructions without any hassle or "back-talk." In other words, they obeyed me. They were not a burden; I enjoyed my time with them very much.

Unfortunately, I had a few of the other kinds of baby-sitting experiences in which there was little joy and a great deal of burden. These were situations in which the children were unruly and disobedient. What a difference obedience or disobedience can make in the life of a baby-sitter—and a servant leader!

6. *That would be of no advantage to you.* When a follower becomes a burden to a leader, everyone is a loser. No one is a winner. The author of Hebrews shares it this way. "Obey them so that their work will be a joy, not a burden, for that would be of no advantage to you" (v. 17). That is true!

There are many ways in which followers can become a burden to a leader. But that kind of activity is of no advantage to the follower; nor is it of any advantage to a leader. No one gains anything. Instead, everyone loses something. When the people of God obey their servant leaders who love them and who are committed to watching over them and to building them up, there is an atmosphere of joy and blessing!

WINNING GOD'S APPROVAL

One of the greatest temptations we face as servant leaders is that of wanting the approval of other people—especially those who are following our leadership. Parents deal with this temptation constantly as do pastors, teachers and Christian employers. Paul faced that concern in his relationship to the Christians in Galatia. He wrote to them, "Am I now trying to win the approval of men, or of God? Or am I trying to please men? If I were still trying to please men, I would not be a servant of Jesus Christ" (Galatians 1:10).

Paul had a remarkable ability to "cut through" an issue to expose the heart of the problem. The people in the churches in Galatia were being led astray by false teachers. They were being influenced by leaders who were not servant leaders of Jesus Christ. Instead those leaders had their own agendas. They were concerned about building their own kingdoms. Paul called the Galatian Christians back to God and back to truth. He exerted his responsibility as their servant leader. He loved them. He had founded their churches. He had led most of them to personal faith in Christ. And he was not going to let them be led astray by false shepherds.

As he addressed them very directly by disciplining them verbally, he re-established his credentials as a servant leader. First, he demonstrated that he was not attempting to win the approval of people by compromising the truth. Instead, he was concerned about winning the approval of God.

Secondly, he contended that he was not concerned with attempting to please men. In fact, he reminded them that if this were his purpose, he could not be a servant of Jesus Christ. His point was an important one—we cannot be functioning as true servants of Jesus Christ if we are seeking to please men or win their approval. We need to go back to the basic teaching of Jesus when he declared, "You cannot serve two masters" (Matthew 6:24).

It is the ultimate purpose of servant leaders to love the persons who are following them, to encourage them to follow Jesus and to build them up so that they are growing to become spiritually mature. This is exactly what Paul was willing to do for the Galatian Christians.

He knew that his greatest gift to them would be to teach them the truth—to call them to accountability. His greatest act of love would be to tell them where they were going the wrong way and to call them back to Jesus. His most important credential was that he was a servant of Jesus Christ. He would not give that up for anybody or anything—not even for the approval of the Galatians.

What a lesson this is for us to learn. To understand that our highest calling and our greatest achievement in life is to be a servant of Jesus Christ. Paul introduced himself as a "servant of Jesus Christ" in most of his epistles. And so did Peter and James. And so should we. It is our highest honor—to be servants of Jesus Christ!

CHAPTER 10

SERVANT LEADERSHIP:

Some Important Dos and Don'ts

In the natural world, leaders exalt themselves. The key descriptive word is "pride"! They "push" and "press" and "politic" in order to gain personal power and recognition. In the kingdom of our Lord, those tactics lead to certain failure.

Though I am free and belong to no man,
I make myself a servant to everyone,
to win as many as possible.
—1 Corinthians 9:19

THE INVITATION TO FOLLOW JESUS CHRIST IS EX-
tended to every person regardless of nationality, color
of skin or economic position. God is no respecter of
persons. But God never coerces anyone to become a
part of his family. The choice is ours!

The same principle applies when a person consid-
ers becoming a servant leader. God invites many of us
to assume that role and responsibility, but he does not
force us to accept his invitation. Just as he invited the
rich young leader to enter his kingdom, he gave him
the opportunity to accept or refuse. Unfortunately,
the young man decided that he loved his money too
much to give it up. He was a "servant" or "slave" of
his money. And his life demonstrated the teaching of
Jesus that we can't serve two masters. So he refused
Jesus' invitation and walked away from Jesus (Mark
10:17–23).

Paul told us that he was a truly free man but
because of his love for Christ and for people, he
became a servant or "willing slave" to people every-
where so that he might win them to Christ.

The way of the "servant" is still our basic model as servant leaders; it is our choice. In his excellent book, *The Celebration of Discipline*, Richard Foster describes clearly what it means to be a servant or a slave by choice:

"But when we choose to be a servant we give up the right to be in charge. There is a great freedom in this. If we voluntarily choose to be taken advantage of, then we cannot be manipulated. When we choose to be a servant we surrender the right to decide who and when we will serve. We become available and vulnerable.

". . . Consider the perspective of a slave. A slave sees all of his life from the viewpoint of slavery. He does not see himself as possessing the same rights as free men and women. Please understand me, when this slavery is involuntary it is cruel and dehumanizing. When the slavery is freely chosen, however, everything is changed. Voluntary servitude is a great joy."[11]

SERVING PEOPLE

As we have seen, love is the basic motive for servant leaders. Such leaders see not merely "tasks," they see "people." They have "long-range" goals along with their "short-range" strategy. One of those long-range goals is to enable people to grow to maturity—to become just as effective as possible in whatever God has created them to be and in whatever he has called them to do.

Paul declared that, his "short-range" strategy was to win as many people as possible for the kingdom of Christ. Therefore, he was willing to become a servant of every person who came into his life with the purpose of winning them for Christ (1 Corinthians 1:9).

Paul's servant leadership role seems different than some of the traditional leadership roles that many of us fill (i.e., as a pastor who becomes the servant of a given flock, or as a Sunday school teacher who assumes the role of being servant to a class of junior high school girls, or as a mother who is called to serve her husband and three children).

Yet the basic principle that Paul gives us is appropriate for all true servant leaders. It is the commitment to become all things to all people so that by all means we might save some (1 Corinthians 9:27). Now, just what did Paul mean by that commitment? The answer to this question, I believe, is in Paul's own life strategy. When he was with the Jews, he attempted to serve them as a fellow Jew. He was sensitive to their customs and ways of doing things. When he was with those who were not under the law, he attempted to serve them appropriately.

And when he was with the weak, he served them as weak. How much this sounds like Mother Teresa, that frail, gentle servant of Christ who has ministered so lovingly to the poor people of Calcutta. Paul was striving to become whatever he needed to become without compromising his Christian integrity. He had the specific goal of winning others for Christ.

Every servant leader needs lofty goals like that. If we do not have them, we will fall into the trap of becoming "self-serving" rather than "God-serving." Servant leaders do not merely serve other people— they don't allow other people to "use" them or to take undue advantage of them. They serve the person and purposes of God.

Paul summarized this truth well when he wrote, "For we do not preach ourselves, but Jesus Christ as Lord, and ourselves as your servants for Jesus' sake" (2 Corinthians 4:5). Ultimately, that is why we become servants of others and servant leaders—for Jesus' sake! We are not advancing our own agenda nor that of anyone else. We are attempting to know and do the will of God ourselves—and then to encourage and enable others to do the same.

We do not preach ourselves. That is, we don't merely communicate our own ideas and preferences. Nor do we strive to build a personal kingdom. Again, we must be warned that servant leaders do not become involved in advancing themselves even though they continually face that subtle temptation.

I have encountered that temptation frequently in my own ministry. Interestingly enough, I find that the particular temptation for self-advancement appears most frequently when things don't seem to be going very well or when I feel that others are not following me or when I am not appreciated as I think I should be.

In our insecurity, all of us are tempted to construct our own agenda which will allow us to gain control of a given situation or of the people whom we are attempting to lead. That is the "natural" thing to do.

However, in the Lord's kingdom, the strategy is quite different. When servant leaders are uncertain or insecure or when they feel they have lost their way, they recognize the need to seek the Lord with all of their hearts. God is the source of our leadership, our love, and our power. And he is the one who needs to establish the direction in which we should be leading. In other words, servant leaders need to be leaders who pray and seek the Lord for guidance. They need to live in constant communion and communication with their leader. They can lead others only as they follow Christ.

It is not a sign of failure or weakness to admit we do not know the way or recognize the next step we should take. Frankly, I find myself in that position quite frequently. Recently, I became very concerned that we provide better pastoral care for the thousands of people who are a part of the Lake Avenue Congregational Church family. I did not know just what to do. I knew what had been effective in other churches that I had pastored. And I had received some helpful information and insights from fellow pastors and sister churches who had solved the basic challenge we were facing.

Yet, at this point, the Lord had not "broken in" to my heart and mind in giving direction in the way in which he would have me to go. Therefore, I shared my concern with the pastoral team and the church family. I invited them to join me in praying and seeking the will of the Lord. I promised them that I would not attempt to move or to lead the congregation until I was certain the Lord had given us his direction. In short, our goal was to know and to do his will!

As you may guess, God answered our prayer in a most remarkable way. We formed a planning task force which led the entire congregation in an All-Church Planning process. The Lord led us in reaching some important conclusions and as a result we agreed upon the appropriate strategy. At this time, we are well on the way to providing much more effective pastoral care. The Lord answered our prayers as we sought his guidance and his will!

I believe that God always will be faithful in answering such prayers. He longs to lead us and guide us if we only give him the opportunity to do so! If we are to be effective as servant leaders, we must continually invite others to join us in seeking the will of God.

As we give this kind of leadership to others, we will face the specific challenge of pride. There are usually some critics who would like us to feel guilty or inadequate when we do not know the way in which we should go. They equate uncertainty with the failure of leadership. Most of us have been reared in a society in which leaders often "fake it" because they believe that leaders should always know what to do and where to go. In addition, our rational society would suggest that any competent leader should be able to "reason" and logically determine the best course to follow.

It is not so with the kingdom of God. As servant leaders, our commitment needs to be to lead where God leads—to follow his direction! We would do well to choose the old gospel song as our theme song, "Where He leads me I will follow!" Friends, if we do not know where he is leading, let us not move until we are certain of his direction.

I believe we would be wise to act like Moses who waited for God's cloud by day and his pillar of fire by night. Or like Gideon who put his fleece before the Lord to be certain that he was doing the will of God. Or like Noah who sent out the dove after the flood to be certain it was God's time for him and the others to leave the ark. Or like Jesus who agonized in the garden seeking to know and to do his Father's will.

PRIDE VS. HUMILITY

Let us acknowledge when we are tempted to be proud, when we are tempted to hide our sin rather than to confess it—or when we pretend to know the way even when we don't! With God's enabling power, let us admit our weakness and acknowledge our constant need to be dependent upon the Lord who alone knows all things—past, present and future. Let us admit that God does not always give us the rationale or the "why" of human events. As he did with Job, the Lord asks us to trust him with all of our hearts and to lean not upon our own understanding. He then encourages us to acknowledge him in all our ways. And, as we do, he has promised to direct our steps (Proverbs 3:5, 6).

That is a basic model for seeking God's guidance
and direction. *Pride* tells us to go it alone; God tells
us to go with him. Pride tells us to follow our instincts;
God tells us to follow him. Pride tells us to utilize
human knowledge and rational approaches; God tells
us to acknowledge him. Pride tells us to "fake it"; God
tells us to allow the truth to set us free. Pride tells us
never to appear weak or uncertain; God tells us that
his strength is made perfect in our weakness. Pride
tells us to have people focus upon us; God tells us to
invite people to follow us with their eyes upon Jesus!

The Lord tells us that pride comes before a fall,
and that they who exalt themselves, will be humbled.
The Book of Proverbs provides this very strong warning, "The Lord detests all the proud of heart. Be sure
of this: They will not go unpunished" (16:5). God
hates pride; it is an abomination to him.

In contrast, the Lord loves the humble. The spirit
of the servant leader is to be humility. The Lord
declares that "those who humble themselves shall be
exalted" (Luke 14:11). The Word of God also contends that "God opposes the proud, but gives grace
to the humble" (James 4:6). James also shares this
wonderful promise, "Humble yourselves before the
Lord, and he will lift you up" (4:10).

In the natural world, leaders exalt themselves.
The key descriptive word is "pride"! They "push"
and "press" and "politic" to gain personal power and
recognition. In the kingdom of our Lord, those tactics lead to certain failure. God instructs servant
leaders to "humble themselves" before him. It is our

responsibility to do that. It is God's business to exalt and promote those of his choosing within his kingdom. To be great in God's kingdom is to be a humble servant of Jesus Christ.

THE SERVANT LEADER IS KIND AND GENTLE

The servant leader is to be not only humble; he or she is also to be kind and gentle. Paul shares this teaching with young Timothy when he writes, "And the Lord's servant must not quarrel; instead he must be kind to everyone, able to teach, not resentful. Those who oppose him he must gently instruct in the hope that God will grant them repentance leading them to a knowledge of the truth" (2 Timothy 2:24, 25).

Within this pithy passage, Paul shares several additional principles of servant leadership. First, one should not quarrel with others. Most of us who have leadership gifts have learned to be effective "persuaders." Often, we get our own way simply by overpowering others with our words and arguments. Paul states that such tactics are not an option for the true servant leader.

I witnessed a vivid example of this approach a number of years ago when I was a young theological student in Chicago. The seminary which I was attending arranged a debate during the famous "God is dead" controversy. A leading Evangelical scholar faced one of the liberal proponents of the "God is dead" theology.

The Evangelical scholar shared solid biblical truth, but he communicated with angry, hostile words and with a confrontive attitude. At the same time, the liberal theologian, who had little viable content, was a kind and gracious man. He spoke with love and respect toward his Evangelical opponent. In my opinion, he lost the debate badly in the area of content. However, he won the hearts of many of the young theologs simply because of his gracious, respectful attitude.

What an important lesson that was for me to learn early in my ministry. It is not enough merely to be orthodox and correct in our doctrine. We must be Christlike in our conduct. A servant leader not only believes the truth; he lives it! He does not quarrel.

And, although this text does not specifically say so, neither does the servant leader flee from his adversaries. Psychologists tell us that most of us respond to negative situations in one of two ways: either "fight" or "flight." Paul tells us that we should not fight with those who oppose us. But neither should we flee. Instead, we should gently instruct those who oppose us. What a marvelous model that is for servant leaders. We do not fight; we do not run. Instead, we seek gently to instruct our opponents with the hope and prayer that God will work in their hearts and that he will bring them to repentance. Our goal should be that they will understand the truth, and that they will escape the trap of the devil. What a strategy!

It is not a matter of my winning and others losing. That is not the point. Instead, it is a matter of all of us winning. Our focus is upon what is best for the other person. It is always best for them to know and understand the truth, and then to follow God's way. As they do, they will escape from the trap of the evil one. When we offer that kind of leadership, everyone involved is blessed greatly.

May I suggest that the next time we find ourselves becoming angry with someone we are trying to lead—or when we feel the urge to fight or flee—let us try God's strategy. Let us humble ourselves and act as a servant leader. Let us try lovingly, patiently and gently to instruct the person who desires to go the wrong way. In other words, let's use God's strategy. Let us minister with his love and wisdom and grace. Let's do it God's way!

Paul also instructs us to be kind to everyone (2 Timothy 2:24). On the natural level, people tend to look at kindness and gentleness as expressions of weakness. Instead, they are expressions of great strength. In fact, I am convinced that most of us cannot use kindness and gentleness effectively without the enabling power of the Holy Spirit. Anyone can fight and quarrel or even flee, but only a person under the control of the Holy Spirit can meet opposition with kindness and gentleness.

In addition, we should not be resentful. It is easy to hold grudges against people who have opposed us. If nothing else, we tend to avoid such persons. That, of course, is a way of "fleeing." Paul says that our strategy as servants of Christ should be that of teaching the truth with kindness and gentleness. I find that many so-called Christians are rude, confrontive, vindictive and condemning. That is not the spirit of Christ. A servant leader is loving, kind and gentle.

The spirit of Christ is the spirit of love—and the spirit of a genuine servant leader is the same. Paul's earlier instruction in this passage is that we should pursue righteousness, faith, love and peace (2 Timothy 2:22). All of those are characteristics of a servant leader. They reflect the character of our leader—Jesus Christ our Lord. Again, the major topic of this chapter comes clearly into focus. We serve Jesus Christ willingly. We are his servants by choice. And, as he has invited us to be servant leaders in his kingdom, we have responded as we have been motivated by his love and grace.

CHAPTER 11

SERVANT LEADERSHIP:

Putting It All Together

. . . servant leadership is not natural; it requires the supernatural—the very presence and power of God!

SERVANT LEADERSHIP IS NOT EASY; NOR IS IT NATURAL. But every one of us can learn to become effective servant leaders. This book is not meant to be a comprehensive presentation of this exciting leadership style. But I have attempted to share some important principles regarding what servant leadership is all about and some basic instructions regarding how you can become a servant leader. I believe that if you prayerfully follow the guidelines of this book, you will be well on your way to becoming an effective servant leader.

Like any spiritual discipline of life, the change will not take place instantly. But we can become servant leaders one step at a time as we submit ourselves to Jesus Christ as Lord, receive the grace and gifting of the Holy Spirit moment by moment, and apply the servant leadership principle of his Word to our daily lives. The principles of this book have come from the Scriptures. In closing let me summarize some of those major principles with you to be used as a checklist of eight specific steps we can take to become effective servant leaders.

1. *All Christians need to understand the principles of servant leadership.* Everyone of us is called to be a servant of Jesus Christ and of others. Most of us are called to be leaders in various life situations. We need to practice servant leadership. The Chief Shepherd is looking over our shoulders. He longs to help us and encourage us in this important task of leading in his way—by his power and love. All leadership by Christians should be servant leadership!

2. *Servant leadership begins with our attitude.* We need to lead with the very attitude of Jesus Christ who made himself nothing and took upon himself the very nature of a servant. This is not natural to any of us. For our attitude to be that of a servant, we need to surrender to Jesus Christ as Lord. His attitude needs to become ours. Before such an attitude becomes ours, the Lord must often lead us into a "desert experience" as he did Moses and Paul and many others—even Jesus. If we are to lead as servants, our hearts must be filled and controlled by Jesus Christ in the person of the Holy Spirit. Servant leadership begins with our attitude!

3. *Love is essential for servant leadership.* Love is central to authentic Christian lifestyle, and it is central in the life of a servant leader. This love needs to begin with our very attitude—it must be our motive for leading. Then it must be translated into our leadership style and activity. As the apostle John declared, "Dear children, let us not love with words or

tongue but with actions and in truth" (1 John 3:18). This active love of Jesus Christ is accompanied by all the fruit of the Spirit including joy, peace and patience. A leader possessed with those attractive qualities is not difficult to follow. He or she uses the power of leadership to lovingly build up the lives of those who follow—not for personal gain or the fulfillment of ego. Servant leaders are lovers, givers and builders!

4. *Biblical models teach us how to be servant leaders.* We have presented several key biblical models which show us both what servant leadership should be and then how to do it! It is a part of the very character of God not merely to tell us *what* we should do—but to give us clear guidelines regarding *how* we should do it. Of course, he gives us the presence and the power of the Holy Spirit to enable us to do it. Also, God has graciously given us role models in our lives who have shown us what servant leadership is all about. Although these models are not perfect, they help point the way toward the practice of authentic servant leadership in our lives. God has given us the perfect model of a servant leader in Jesus Christ. When we receive him as our Savior and follow him as our Lord, he provides a model of servant leadership for us that is without comparison. He invites us to live as he lived, to minister as he ministered, to lead as he led—as servant leaders.

5. *The role of the Good Shepherd helps us understand what it means to be a servant leader.* Jesus used the example of a good shepherd to help us understand the qualities and practices of an effective

servant leader. That same metaphor of a good shepherd is used extensively in both the Old and New Testaments. Three of the major contributions of a good shepherd are: (a) A good shepherd knows his or her sheep; (b) a good shepherd is willing to lay down his or her life for the sheep; and (c) a good shepherd leads the sheep. In the same way, servant leaders need to know the people entrusted to their care, to be willing to risk and be inconvenienced—even to literally laying down our lives—for the people we are leading, and to lead the sheep where God wants them to be led—to do the will of God.

6. *Servant leaders must know how to be servant followers.* None of us is exclusively a servant leader. All of us also have the role of being servant followers. The Lord calls us to be obedient. In fact, obedience is the key to Christian discipleship. That is what faith is all about—active obedience. God wants us to obey him and the leaders whom he entrusts to us. The Scripture declares that we should submit to the authority of our leaders—even kings and rulers. We should allow leadership to be a joy to them. It is to our advantage to do so. Effective servant leaders must first be effective servant followers.

7. *Servant leaders are accountable to God.* To be a servant leader is not only a privilege, it is an awesome responsibility. James says that we would be judged by God with greater strictness than others who are only followers. Peter declares that the Chief Shepherd, Jesus Christ, will someday reward us according to our track record. There is no such thing as

servant leadership within the kingdom of God which lacks accountability. Therefore, we should be careful to follow the Lord with all of our hearts and minds and strength. And we should invite others to follow us only as we are following Jesus as Lord!

8. *Servant leaders must lead by choice.* Servant leadership goes far beyond a quality of leadership that merely responds to a legal responsibility or a religious duty. God wants us to lead willingly and eagerly. The highest calling of a servant leader is to serve God and then to serve the people entrusted to his care. Servant leaders are tempted to be motivated by pride. Instead, God helps us to become humble—like Jesus and to lead with kindness and gentleness.

A FINAL CHALLENGE

You can be a servant leader whether you are a parent or a pastor or a Sunday school teacher or a little league coach—or a small group Bible study leader. Whatever your leadership role may be, the Lord desires for you to be a servant leader.

Our human temptation is to critique others. It would be natural to take the material from this book to use as a checklist for finding the shortcomings of the leaders in our lives. Our parents would probably not meet the test, nor our pastors, nor our employers—nor a number of other significant leaders in our lives. This is not the point; it is not the purpose of this book.

Instead, we need to use the checklist to compare the principles of servant leadership with our own lives and leadership styles. As we do so, our purpose should not be to condemn or pass judgment upon ourselves. On the contrary, the purpose of this book is to encourage and enable us to take specific steps toward becoming effective servant leaders ourselves. Harry Gladstone, John Steelman and Mary Alvarez are examples of people like us who learned how to become servant leaders. We can do it too!

We need to be encouraged that we are not alone in this worthy pursuit. Other Christian brothers and sisters are learning and growing with us. For example, I would encourage you to find a group of people in your church who would like to become effective servant leaders. You may begin with your pastor. Allow him to lead you and others in a study of this book and the various biblical passages which we have presented to you. As you do, use the checklist to assist you in taking specific steps toward servant leadership.

Above all, we know that the Lord is anxious to help us in this important venture. He was not left us alone. He longs to empower and encourage us as we follow Jesus as Lord and as the Holy Spirit controls our life and enables us to do far beyond what we can do in our own strength and wisdom. Remember, servant leadership is not natural; it requires the supernatural—the very presence and power of God!

You can be a servant leader!

Notes

1. Robert K. Greenleaf, *Servant Leadership* (New York: Paulist Press, 1977), 7.
2. Written by Gordon Aseschliman, Editor of *WORLD CHRISTIAN Magazine*.
3. Russ Reid, "What Ruins Christian Leaders?" *Eternity Magazine*, February, 1981.
4. Bob Toms, Excerpt from an address at ESEC chapel service (used with permission).
5. Robert Mitchell, Excerpt from letter dated August, 1982 (used with permission).
6. Dr. Robert Saucy, Excerpt from a lecture on Servant Leadership (used with permission).
7. Robert K. Greenleaf, *Servant Leadership* (New York: Paulist Press, 1977) 13–14.
8. Clyde Reid, *Pastoral Psychology*, Vol. 19, No. 183, April, 1968.
9. Pei-Lu Liu, excerpt from a letter (used with permission).
10. Hans Küng, *The Church* (New York: Sheed and Ward, 1967), 401.
11. Richard Foster, *Celebration of Discipline* (Harper and Row, 1978), 115–116.

STUDY GUIDE

MAKING STRESS

WORK FOR YOU

STUDY GUIDE

Study Guide

Chapter 1. Who Needs It?

Questions:
1. As you begin to read this book, what would be your present understanding of servant leadership? How would you define servant leadership?

2. How do you think that servant leadership could be of help to you?

3. How did Jesus model servant leadership?

4. What seems to be your greatest challenge in becoming a servant leader?

Chapter 2. Where Do We Begin?

Questions:
1. How do you identify with the "desert" experience of Paul Cedar?

2. How would you describe the servant attitude of Jesus?

3. Describe any "desert experience" you have experienced in your own life.

4. How does servant leadership seem to require "swimming against the stream"?

5. What is the importance of one's motive in being a servant leader?

Chapter 3. Love Is Essential

Questions:
1. What is the place of love in servant leadership?

2. Why isn't sincerity adequate in itself to make us servant leaders?

3. What dangers lie in the abuse of power of a leader?

4. What relationship do the "fruit of the Spirit" have with servant leadership?

5. How does a servant leader function as a "builder"?

Chapter 4. Some Biblical Models

Questions:
1. Within what context must servant leadership take place? Why?

2. Outline the model that the apostle Paul has given us for servant leadership in Ephesians 4.

3. How does servant leadership result in unity?

4. Describe Paul's succinct model for servant leadership found in 1 Corinthians 11:1.

5. How do these two models relate to you and your leadership role?

Chapter 5. The Ideal Model!

Questions:

1. How did Jesus model servant leadership to his disciples at his last supper?

2. How did Jesus teach by example?

3. How can we teach by example?

4. Outline the basic teaching of Jesus concerning servant leadership.

5. How was Jesus an example to us in serving and giving?

Chapter 6. A Working Model

Questions:

1. How should we shepherd God's flock?

2. How should we serve willingly?

3. How can we serve eagerly?

4. How can we serve as examples?

Chapter 7. Leading Like a Shepherd

Questions:
1. Why should a shepherd know his or her sheep?

2. Why is it important for the sheep to know the shepherd?

3. How does a good shepherd "lay down his life" for his sheep?

4. How could we "lay down our lives" for the people we lead?

5. Why is it vital for servant leaders not to attempt to "own" or "control" those whom they lead?

Chapter 8. A Warning to Bad Leaders

Questions:
1. What happens when a servant leader fails to lead?

2. What warning does God give to leaders who care only for themselves?

3. What are some of the potential pitfalls faced by servant leaders?

4. What seems to be your greatest failure as a servant leader?

5. What are you going to do about it to overcome that failure?

Chapter 9. Leaders and Followers

Questions:
1. Who is called to be a follower?

2. How can we become effective followers?

3. How should followers obey their leaders?

4. What responsibility does a servant leader have to his followers?

5. How do servant leaders win God's approval?

Chapter 10. Some Important Dos and Don'ts

Questions:
1. What leadership principles did the apostle Paul practice?

2. How can those principles be of help to us?

3. How does humility relate to servant leadership?

4. How should a servant leader practice kindness and gentleness?

5. How are you "measuring up" in serving with humility, kindness and gentleness?

Chapter 11. Putting It All Together

Questions:
1. How will change take place in our lives as we apply the principles of servant leadership?

2. What are the eight specific steps we can take to become effective servant leaders?

3. Which steps have you taken (or are in the process of taking)?

4. Which steps seem to be most difficult for you to take?

5. How is Jesus Christ the most important key to us in becoming servant leaders?

Bibliography

Barrs, Jerram. *Shepherds and Sheep: A Biblical View of Leading and Following.* Illinois: InterVarsity Press, 1983.

Dayton, Edward R. and Engstrom, Ted W. *Strategy for Leadership.* New Jersey: Fleming Revell Company, 1979.

Eims, LeRoy. *Be the Leader You Were Meant to Be.* Illinois: SP Publications, Inc., 1975.

Erwin, Gayle D. *The Jesus Style.* Waco, Texas: Word Books, 1986.

Foster, Richard J. *Celebration of Discipline: The Path to Spiritual Growth.* San Francisco: Harper & Row, 1978.

Greenleaf, Robert K. *Servant Leadership.* New York: Paulist Press, 1977.

Smith, Fred. *Learning to Lead.* Waco, Texas: Word Books, 1986.

Swindoll, Charles R. *Improving Your Serve.* Waco, Texas: Word Books, 1981.

———. *Leadership.* Waco, Texas: Word Books, 1985.

PAUL A. CEDAR is senior pastor of Lake Avenue Congregational Church in Pasadena, California. Also founder of Dynamic Communications, Inc., he serves as its president; it is a nonprofit ministry to pastors and churches. Among Dr. Cedar's previous books are *Seven Keys to Maximum Communication*, *Sharing the Good Life* and *James, 1 and 2 Peter and Jude* in *The Communicator's Commentary*. Cedar earned his doctorate in ministry from American Baptist Seminary of the West. He also attended Northern Baptist Theological Seminary, Wheaton College and Trinity Evangelical Divinity School. He served as Dean of the Billy Graham School of Evangelism from 1983–85. He also served as Adjunct Professor at Fuller Theological Seminary and Talbot Theological Seminary and Visiting Professor of Evangelism at Trinity Evangelical Divinity School.